WHATSOEVER YOU SHALL

ASK IN PRAYER

BELIEVING, YOU SHALL RECEIVE.
MATTHEW 21:22

A FAITH-PROMOTING JOURNEY

TOM BOWERS

To Will

Thankyou for being
a faithful companion a scout the
Camp. Have fun discovering the
secret joys of this book.

Tom
8/11/19

PREFACE

IN JANUARY 2015, while I was having lunch with the president of the Manhattan Temple of the Church of Jesus Christ of Latter-day Saints,[1] he asked me about my conversion to the Church. In response, I related some of the stories included in this book. He encouraged me to write them down. His support seemed like a mandate from God to do so.

Up to that point, I only had a few notes on incidents that seemed unrelated to each other. With the help of friends and editors, I have created a coherent storyline. My intention in writing this book is to provide an empowering account of my spiritual journey. Another purpose is to inspire you, the reader, to find your own stories waiting to be told.

Throughout the creative process, my wife has been my partner. Her support has touched my heart, and our relationship has deepened. Our son and daughter have contributed by cheering me on to completion. Thanks to the following friends and editors my story has come to life: Ionut Epure, Chip Hughes, Katie Olsen, Thomas Ward, Rebecca Hunt Monson, Olivia Swenson, Micky Chorny, Deborah Dove, and Catherine Dunn.

My participation in the Landmark Forum, a personal development seminar, empowered me to finish this book. Before that three-and-a-half-day course, I had stopped writing. I was uncomfortable putting myself at the center of attention. During the Landmark Forum, I saw my story could be whatever I created it to be. I found the freedom to put aside my concern my story was about me. I was then able to complete my account as an expression of my gratitude to God for His abiding love.

I dedicate this book to my Heavenly Father, who leads me, guides me, and walks beside me.

Notes:

1. The Church of Jesus Christ of Latter-day Saints issued the following statement from President Russell M. Nelson on August 16, 2018, regarding the name of the Church: "The Lord has impressed upon my mind the importance of the name He has revealed for His Church, even The Church of Jesus Christ of Latter-day Saints." In keeping with the style guide published at the time of the announcement, I use the full name of the Church or refer to it as "the Church" rather than use the terms "Mormon Church" or "LDS Church." When I refer to members of the Church, I use "Latter-day Saints" or "Latter-day Saint" rather than "Mormons" or "Mormon" with few exceptions.

CHAPTER 1

MY PRAYER TO BE AMAHL

MY SIXTH-GRADE CHOIR director called me out of class to meet with her. She asked me if I would like to audition for the part of Amahl in the Christmas musical, *Amahl and the Night Visitors*.[1] The role called for a boy with a soprano voice, and she thought it was a good fit for me. The prospect of being in a musical thrilled me. The day before the tryout, my choir director played the grand piano in our school auditorium as I stood and sang the song she had chosen for the audition. She coached me to sing with feeling and confidence.

I wanted the part and wondered what more I could do to get it. I could pray! In the bathroom in our home, I locked the door to be alone and knelt on the beige tiled floor. I put my hands together, bowed my head and reverently asked out loud, "Heavenly Father, please give me the part of Amahl." Confident God had heard my prayer, and I would get the part, I sang for the selection committee.

The part went to another boy. My disappointment left me wondering why God had not answered my prayer. I knew God answered prayers. What went wrong?

Two months later, my mother met a woman who was a singing teacher and asked me if I would like to take voice lessons. I enthusiastically accepted her offer. Winifred, my singing coach, had moved to our town of Oroville, California after I had offered my prayer. I told her about my audition, and she said she planned to produce *Amahl and the Night Visitors* the following Christmas. God had heard my prayer.

For more than six months, she prepared me for the role of Amahl. As the performance drew near, I rehearsed with the cast and orchestra for weeks. When the curtain went up on the stage in the local municipal auditorium, I was ready.

The character of Amahl used a crutch to walk. When the three kings stopped for the night at his home, he discovered they were taking gifts to the Christ child. He wanted to send his own gift. As Amahl extended his crutch as his offering, he took a step. To his surprise and the delight of everyone, he could walk. The entire cast celebrates in song his miraculous healing. First, the kings, then his mother, then everyone on stage joins in: "He walks!" The music builds to a crescendo in joyous celebration of the miracle of Amahl's healing. What a thrill to be part of the depiction of the miraculous power of a simple act of giving! The story ends as Amahl goes with the wise men on their journey to find the Prince of Peace.

A year earlier when I had prayed earnestly to be cast in the role of Amahl, the Lord had heard me. In His own way and in His own time, He answered my prayer. I had exercised my faith, trusted in God, and poured out my heart to Him. In the end, He validated my belief that there is power in prayer.

I could relate to Amahl. His need for a crutch reminded me of my injury when I was nine. Dad had come home with a new horse named Thunder. He was high-strung and moody; his name fit him well. A few weeks later, I went to the barn to feed the horses. I found Thunder in the hay storage area gorging himself. Other horses had broken in to feed on the bailed hay, and I knew what to do.

I took Thunder by his halter, led him out of the barn, and closed the door. Unaware he was enraged, I turned my back on him and started walking to the house. He took aim, reared up on his front legs, and kicked me on both sides of my tail bone, sending me airborne. The impact left me stunned and disoriented.

When I could stand, I hobbled back to the house in pain. My mother examined me for injuries and only found horseshoe-shaped bruises on my butt. There was no external bleeding, and I didn't seem to have any broken bones. Mom didn't see any need to take me to a doctor, and I just dealt with the pain by sitting on a pile of pillows. In two weeks, the bruises disappeared, and I thought the effect of the incident was over.

In reality, the impact of the horse's kick had injured my spine. My muscles constricted around the injury and shortened my right leg. My entire spinal alignment was twisted by the torque of the blow. I didn't walk with a noticeable limp, but I stood with my right shoulder lower than my left.

Being kicked also left me with emotional stress. Soon after the Thunder incident, I reacted to my fourth-grade teacher's instructions by blurting out, "I will do it my way, and I don't need your help." This defiant attitude surprised me. I had never said anything like that to anyone before. That was the first of many emotional reactions, and I stifled them as much as I could.

Oroville, where I was living when Thunder kicked me and I performed in the Christmas musical, became my childhood home in 1955 when I was six. Before that, I lived on our farm and orchard in Santa Clara, California, with my parents, my sister Claudia, and my brother Dan. My father was born on the farm, and his parents still lived there. My mother's father, Grandpa Appelbe, bought a plot of land from Grandpa Bowers after my parents married and built a house on it so he and Grandma Appelbe could be near us. We were within an easy bike ride of both sets of grandparents. As children, we loved dropping in on them.

Grandma Bowers spoiled us with chocolate chips and spoonfuls of brown sugar. If we were careful not to scratch the bench on her huge Hammond organ, she would let us press the keys and pedals. The best part of our visits was when she read to us. With full attention, we listened to her read Bible stories. Her faith in the miraculous works of God was evident as she recreated those sacred events.

The accounts of Daniel inspired me. He was my hero because he refused to defile himself by eating the king's food, and he interpreted the handwriting on the wall. I was left with a deep impression of Daniel's close connection to God, and his commitment to getting down on his knees in prayer three times a day. To my amazement, Daniel kept praying even when King Darius outlawed prayer to God, threatening death as the punishment to anyone who defied his edict. Upon hearing the terms of the new law, Daniel went home and knelt in prayer with his windows open. I often thought about Daniel praying in spite of the threat to his life. The power he found in prayer was on my mind when I prayed to get the part of Amahl.

Grandpa Bowers was in his seventies and in poor health when we lived in Santa Clara, but he still made time for me. One day when we were in the yard, he had a pair of binoculars with him. We walked side by side under the tall evergreens surrounding his home. We could see the Lick Observatory on top of Mount Hamilton in the distance. Standing in the farmyard, he carefully took the binoculars out of the case, put the strap around my neck, and handed them to me. I looked into the binoculars, and to my surprise, the observatory appeared to be right in front of me. That brief incident serves as a fond memory of his love for me.

I loved visiting Grandpa and Grandma Appelbe as well. They had emigrated from England in their youth. In keeping with her English heritage, Grandma Appelbe would sit us down in her kitchen for a cup of tea with milk. It was great! Grandpa Appelbe was a retired contractor who had built custom homes. He kept the tools of his trade in his garage. After showing me how to make a hole in a piece of wood, he handed me the drill. I cranked the handle, and I made my own hole. We bonded in the process.

After my father made some prudent business transactions—including trading most of the farm in what is now Silicon Valley for a fruit orchard in Gridley, California—we moved to Oroville. In the process, he transformed himself into a real estate developer and a major fruit grower. The combination of farming and commercial real estate provided financial security for our family.

All four of my grandparents followed us. My father's parents moved to Gridley, about twelve miles away, and Grandpa Appelbe built a house on the property behind our home to be as close as possible to his grandchildren. Even though I missed the familiar surroundings of our farm in Santa Clara, the move was easier because my grandparents moved with us.

My mother took us to the Methodist Church every Sunday. Ducking out was never an option. In my preteen years, her firm commitment to take us to church always won over my inclination to stay home and watch TV in my pajamas. At night she would sit by my side and coach me in memorizing Bible passages such as the Twenty-third Psalm and the Lord's Prayer. The sacred words, "Goodness and mercy shall follow me all the days of my life: and I will dwell in the house of the Lord forever" (Psalms 23:6) became my expectation.

Dad was a silent partner in Mom's quest to establish religion in our lives. For Dad, going to church was an ordeal. When he did attend, he would wince if anyone sang off-key, and only a rare humorous sermon could keep him awake. However, he showed where his heart was by giving generously. One day a member of the Methodist Church came to our home and asked Dad for a donation for the building fund. Without hesitation, he wrote a check to the Methodist Church for one thousand dollars. As Dad handed over his gift, I was proud he was supporting the church.

I served as an acolyte from the time I was eight until I was twelve. Just before the church service began, I put on a white-and-black cassock and reverently walked down the main aisle of the sanctuary carrying a long, lighted pole to illuminate the candles on the altar. Above the altar was a beautiful stained-glass window portraying Jesus kneeling in the Garden of Gethsemane. He looked heavenward with an earnest, pleading expression. On the front edge of the altar, carved words read, "In Remembrance of Me." With an attitude of worship and reverence, I walked down the aisle and lit the candles on the altar in honor of Jesus Christ as the light of the world. The image of Jesus in the window and the words cut in wood engendered sacred feelings that are permanently engraved on my heart.

In Sunday School, we sang, "Jesus loves me, this I know, for the Bible tells me so."[2] After affirming His love for me in song, I wondered how to connect His love to my daily life. When I got home, the loving feelings I had at church faded into a memory.

After being kicked by Thunder, I often wondered, "Why don't I feel loved?" My parents and grandparents were a constant loving presence in my life. The love of God came through when I attended church, and I had a loving response to my prayer to get the part of Amahl. However, in spite of the love that was all around, I was frequently anxious. Though unrecognized for many years, Thunder's kick was a defining moment and undermined my ability to acknowledge and accept the love extended to me by God and my family.

Notes:

1. Menotti, G. (1962). *Amahl and the Night Visitors*. New York: G. Schirmer.

2. Warner, S., & Warner, A. (1860). *Say and Seal*. Philadelphia, PA: Lippincott & Company.

CHAPTER 2

TRIALS OF AN EAGLE SCOUT

FROM THE TIME I was old enough to be a Boy Scout, I attended weekly troop meetings. Each week we pledged to keep the Scout Oath and Law. On my honor, I gave my word to be trustworthy, loyal, helpful, friendly, courteous, kind, obedient, cheerful, thrifty, brave, clean and reverent. These qualities became the standard for my life.

The closing was my favorite part of our meetings. We gathered in a circle with our arms on each other's shoulders, dimmed the lights, and sang "Taps": "Day is done, gone the sun, From the lakes, from the hills, from the sky; All is well, safely rest, God is nigh."[1] We then raised our right arms in the Scout sign and bowed toward the center of the circle as the senior patrol leader left us with the benediction: "May the Great Scoutmaster of all Scouts be with us until we meet again." I loved the fellowship and the reverence of that moment.

My first summer at Scout camp, my mother sent me a package wrapped in brown paper and tied with string. I had no idea what it was. I opened it and discovered my favorite chocolate chip brownies. What a surprise! Her love was tangibly present as I shared the brownies with my friends. I appreciated her reminder that she was thinking of me.

I progressed quickly through the Scout ranks, and I became a member of the Scout service organization, the Order of the Arrow. I made Native American clothing and joined a dance team.

When I was twelve, tragedy struck. I lost three of my grandparents. Grandma Bowers died in March, Grandpa Appelbe died in April, and Grandpa Bowers died in July. Even though I didn't see my father's parents often after we moved to Oroville, their loss left an emptiness that couldn't be filled.

The death of Grandpa Appelbe was the hardest of all. He was part of my daily life. In the morning, I waited for the school bus near his house and often stopped to see him on my way home. One day when I got sick at school, the principal couldn't reach my mother, and he called my grandfather. Grandpa Appelbe picked me up, brought me to his home, and put me to bed. I knew he loved me, and I loved him.

As a Cub Scout, I asked him to help me make a car for the Pinewood Derby. I didn't know there was a specific kind of car to build. I just thought I was supposed to create a car. Grandpa took me downstairs to his workshop, we found a piece of wood, and we fashioned it into a small car. He helped me cut the wood to size, showed me how to shape it with a chisel, explained the different kinds of sandpaper, and taught me to sand with the grain. We made the wheels from a broom handle and axles from door hinges. I loved that little car we made together.

I didn't know he had a heart problem. He seemed fine to me. I came home one day to find he had died from a heart attack while he was working in his yard. I was in shock. I couldn't cry. I couldn't feel anything. There was nothing to do but carry on.

In May, a few weeks after his death, I performed with my Native American dance team in the Feather Fiesta Days parade. My brother Bert was born a few days earlier. When I got back from the parade, Mom was home from the hospital with my little brother. What a pleasure to hold him for the first time! I joined my family in giving him the love he needed.

Against the backdrop of these changes in my family, my Scouting activities continued. When I was thirteen, the troop went on an unforgettable one-hundred-mile hike through the Sierras. It was an epic trek from Mount Lassen National Park to Bucks Lake. One of the assistant scoutmasters raised homing pigeons. For our hike, he attached a cage atop his backpack and carried several pigeons with him. He released them at different points on the hike to deliver messages to our families. We also had food airdropped at strategic locations so that we didn't have to carry provisions for all seven days. What a memorable week!

Later that year, I became an Eagle Scout. It was a proud moment, and I was eager for more. I discovered there was a religious award in Scouting. In the Methodist Church, it was the God and Country Award. As an expression of "A Scout is Reverent," I worked on the requirements for the award with our minister. I studied the Bible and learned more about the Methodist Church. In doing so, I realized that Christ intends that his followers live in cooperation with each other. With this in mind, I attended membership classes. In those classes, I learned the principle of tithing. I was impressed with the importance of paying a tithe of 10 percent of your income to the church as an offering to God. From then on, I paid a tithe to the church on whatever money I received. I was proud of keeping my commitment to tithing. At the end of the class series, I became a member of the Methodist Church.

Another way I expressed my reverence toward God was by singing in local churches. The song I sang was "The Lord's Prayer."[2] I sang it in the Methodist Church, the Congregational Church, the Episcopalian Church, and the Presbyterian Church. With my heart filled with praise, I sang, "Our Father, which art in heaven. Hallowed be Thy name. Thy kingdom come, Thy will be done in earth as it is in heaven. Give us this day our daily bread and forgive us our debts as we forgive our debtors, and lead us not into temptation, but deliver us from evil. For Thine is the kingdom and the power and the glory forever. Amen." I always had a sacred, holy feeling whenever I sang that song.

From those visits to different churches, I discovered that they all had similar worship services. I felt the same closeness

11

to God in all of them. It seemed odd that people who basically believed the same things worshipped separately.

In February 1963, our council held the annual Scout show at the municipal auditorium in Oroville. Cub packs, Scout troops, and Explorer posts from all over the council filled the auditorium with activity and display booths. While I was staffing our troop's booth with a slide show of our one-hundred-mile hike, the chief Scout executive of our council had a conversation with me. He told me about a tour of Europe for Scouts, which included a visit to the World Jamboree in Marathon, Greece. The previous summer I had applied to be part of the official American contingent to the Jamboree. They returned my application because they had met their quota for Scouts. The possibility of going on the tour re-invigorated my excitement about going to the Jamboree! I asked my parents if I could go. They gave me permission and paid for the trip.

The tour originated in Phoenix, Arizona, with twenty Scouts who came from Arizona, California, and Texas. There was also about the same number of adults, all from the Phoenix area. We traveled in buses and planes to major European cities. The trip changed my life.

The tour included a Presbyterian minister assigned to watch over the Scouts. He noticed I avoided two of the young men who used foul language. He took me aside to hear what I had to say. This minister's care gave me a new understanding of what it meant to have someone care about me. As I got to know him, I could see that he was a people person. Every spare moment, he was writing a postcard to someone back home or giving someone his full attention. I wanted to be like him.

In London, we stayed at the Baden-Powell House, a hostel for Scouts. I fell in love with the place. Scouts were coming and going from all over the world. I determined that one day I would go back and visit again. While we were there, I got to know Erik, who was on the summer staff from Norway, and we promised to write to each other.

During the tour, we visited many cathedrals and religious sites, such as the place where Paul gave his speech on the unknown God in Athens, and the catacombs—tunnels under the city of Rome where Christians worshipped in secret in the first century. The tour had the feel of a religious pilgrimage.

I have enduring impressions of the religious art we saw. Before the trip, art had just been beautiful pictures and statues. On the tour, religious art became something to experience more than just something to see. The first painting that grabbed my attention was a painting of the Savior knocking on a door. The painting entitled *Light of the World* hangs in St. Paul's Cathedral in London. I still remember standing in front of it and pondering the Lord extending His love, in hopes that His knock would be heard and the person within would open the door.

Seeing Michelangelo's *Pieta* in St. Peter's Basilica created another lasting memory. It is a life-like statue carved in marble showing Jesus' mother holding His limp, lifeless body in her arms. The statue awakened feelings of reverence and compassion, and I stood in awe before it. Those sacred feelings return whenever I think back on that moment.

In Greece, we stayed in Athens and took a bus each day to the Jamboree held on the plains of Marathon. The Scout Law includes the statement "a Scout is a friend to all and a brother to every other Scout." As I walked around the Jamboree encampment, those Scouts from all over the world were my brothers. Sometimes it was difficult to communicate because of language differences, but we managed. We traded badges and exchanged addresses. Our time together left me with an enduring sense of brotherhood.

When I returned from the trip, I had different expectations. I was no longer content with the way things had been before the trip. I wanted to have the same warm connection to my family I had with the minister who befriended me. I longed to relive the sacred moments I had with religious art. I was eager to continue to enjoy a sense of brotherhood with Scouts from all over the world.

To awaken the religious feelings I had with art, I hung on my wall a print of a painting of an old woman in prayer. To reconnect to the international brotherhood of Scouts, I corresponded with Scouts in several countries. However, I was not able to regain the connection I had with the minister on the trip with anyone in my family. I even became angry with my mother because she didn't listen to me the way he did.

The trip also changed my expectations for Sunday School. I wanted it to be a place where I could connect to God and expand my understanding of Him. Our class discussions did not leave me with a feeling that God was present, and the Sunday School teacher did not provide engaging answers to my questions. As a result, I stopped attending Sunday School and just participated in congregational worship.

When I was a sophomore in high school, I had a rare moment of connection with my brother Dan, who was two years younger than I. Normally we bickered and put each other down; however, on this occasion he was distressed. I asked him what happened, and he said his male Spanish teacher got him drunk and touched him sexually. He swore me to secrecy; I was powerless to help him in his torment. Soon after he confided in me, he almost killed himself by drinking too much alcohol in a short time. Alcohol was easily accessible in our home. Dad had a liquor cabinet, and there was no lock on it. After his near-death experience, Dan spent several months in a state mental hospital. When we went to see him, I saw what a mental hospital was like—more of a prison than a place to heal. I brooded over Dan's trials, and I wondered about the meaning of life.

During this time of internal struggle, in French class, we read Albert Camus' *L'Etranger*.[3] The main character in the story kills a man for no apparent reason. In prison, he denounces Christianity and refuses to appeal to religion for solace. He concludes that life is meaningless and without rational order. He looks forward to his execution as a confirmation that life is ridiculous. Reading this book was more than a French lesson. I came to the same conclusion as the man in Camus' story—life is meaningless, irrational, and ridiculous.

I kept up a correspondence with Erik, the Norwegian Scout I met at the Baden-Powell House. He encouraged me to apply there to serve as a volunteer. In September 1965, I made a request for a staff position the following summer. Before long, they wrote back to welcome me as part of the 1966 summer staff. Even though I looked forward to returning to the Baden-Powell House, my view of life as meaningless undermined my self-confidence and lingered like a dark shadow.

The following spring, I played the male lead in our high school musical, *Bells Are Ringing*. As I stepped onto the stage as Jeff, I took on his personality, and I experienced myself as this disempowered alcoholic playwright. When the curtain came down, some of the lyrics from the song "Just in Time"[4] stayed with me. The words that stuck in my mind expressed my character's hopelessness before meeting his girlfriend. The song is intended to be a celebration of the transformative effect of her love. I did not have a sense of redemption. I was in despair.

In an attempt to find a caring adult like the minister on my European tour, I developed a friendship with my French teacher. In preparation for my trip to England, I proposed to him that we would travel together on his annual trip to Winnipeg, Canada. It was my idea of how to reduce the cost of airfare to Europe. Flights were cheaper from Winnipeg than California. He said he would be glad to have my company on the trip. I made my proposal to my parents, and they agreed to the plan. Going to Winnipeg would also give me a chance to visit some of my mother's relatives whom I had never met. Once I arrived in Winnipeg, I would fly to Oslo, visit Erik, spend a few days in Copenhagen and Paris, then work the rest of the summer at the Baden-Powell House.

On our trip to Canada, my French teacher and I had long hours to talk. At one point, he went into detail about a sexual adventure he had with another young man in his youth. I told him, "That is not a story for me, and I don't want to hear it." He went on to say that he found me attractive. This was a shock. I had no idea that he was interested in me as a sexual partner.

When we stopped for the night, he got a room with one bed, and I told him, "I am not going to sleep in the same bed with you." I took a blanket and a pillow from the bed, and I slept on the floor. I was furious he had used our trip to reveal his physical attraction to me. Our trip left me angry and resentful toward him. This was not the authentic caring extended to me by the minister on my trip to Europe.

Except for my French teacher's disclosure of his interest in having sex with me, the summer went as planned. I had a great time in Norway, Copenhagen, and Paris. In London, I loved working side by side with Scouts from all over the United Kingdom and Europe in the Baden-Powell House cafeteria. I also enjoyed meeting the Scouts who stayed at the hostel from all over the world.

Scouting provided me with good values and empowering activities in my adolescent years. My quest to fulfill the promise of "A Scout is Reverent" led me to join the Methodist Church and to sing in local churches. To fulfill my declaration that "A Scout is Friendly," I corresponded with Scouts in many parts of the world. In spite of those empowering influences, I was preoccupied with anxiety. My grief over the loss of Grandpa Appelbe, my distress over my brother's troubles, and my resentment toward my French teacher lingered and fostered my view that life was absurd and meaningless.

Notes:

1. Hurd, Rukard. (1878). "Taps." Chester, PA: Pennsylvania Military College.

2. Malotte, A. (1935). "The Lord's Prayer." New York: G. Schirmer.

3. Camus, A. (1942). *L'Etranger*. Paris: Gallimard.

4. Comden, B., & Green, A. (Lyricists). & Styne, J. (Composer). (1956). "Just in Time." From *Bells Are Ringing*. London: Chappell.

CHAPTER 3

BE STILL AND KNOW THAT I AM GOD[1]

I RETURNED FROM England and started my senior year of high school. I didn't tell anyone about the breakdown in my relationship with my French teacher, not even my parents. On my schedule of classes was fourth-year French. If I took the course, I would have to be with my French teacher five days a week. To avoid explaining why I didn't want to take French, I stayed in his class.

During the French lessons, I avoided eye contact with the teacher and only responded if he called on me. My bitterness toward him festered and depleted my energy. I worried I might be sent to a mental hospital. The prospect of being institutionalized terrified me. I had seen what it was like for my brother, and I didn't want that.

Toward the end of September, my distress affected my health, and I contracted a severe case of bronchitis. I took the initiative and went to our family doctor for advice. After I explained the impact of my French teacher's comments, she referred me to a psychotherapist. With his counseling, I was able to calm down and regain a measure of stability. I went to weekly therapy sessions from October 1966 until I graduated from high school the following spring. When I graduated and went off to college, I was still coping with my stressors.

During this time of depression, regular attendance at the Methodist Church provided much-needed support, but I wanted more. My mother had given me a Bible when I was fourteen; I often turned to it for comfort. One verse stood out to me: "Blessed are those who hunger and thirst after righteousness, for they shall be filled" (Matthew 5:6). I longed to be filled as the verse promised.

Over the Christmas break, I had an assignment to read an autobiography for my English class. I went to the public library to look for one. I picked up a small green copy of Benjamin Franklin's autobiography, thumbed through it, and rejected it. The print was small, and there were no pictures. Then I picked up a larger book with blue binding, *Autobiography of a Yogi*. I liked the larger type, and there were lots of photographs. His life as a yogi piqued my interest. I had been reading a book on yoga postures, which included spiritual guidance. One aphorism advised, "In a conflict between your heart and mind, always follow your heart." This statement of truth appealed to me. With the intent of completing my assignment *and* satisfying my curiosity about yoga, I left the library with Paramahansa Yogananda's life story.

I spent my Christmas break enthralled with Yogananda's stories of his encounters with holy men. Before reading his book, I thought saints were historical figures and miracles didn't happen anymore. But his personal accounts created a vivid reality of living saints and contemporary miracles. I formulated a vision for my life of being surrounded by saintly people and blessed with divine manifestations.

At the end of the book, there was an invitation to subscribe to weekly lessons from the organization he founded, the Self-Realization Fellowship. I sent for the lessons, eager to learn more. One lesson at a time, I studied and put into practice Yogananda's teachings. They gave me the focus for my life I was seeking and served as an antidote to my frustrations with the meaninglessness of life.

Central to Yogananda's training is the guru-disciple relationship. Describing his first meeting with his teacher, Yogananda said, "I sensed that my guru knew God and would lead me to Him."[2] I modeled my relationship with Yogananda around the quality of his relationship with his guru. I followed Yogananda confident that under his guidance I would come to know God. Even though Yogananda died in 1952, I developed a personal connection to him.

Yogananda professed that you come to know God by being still. He taught two fundamental meditation techniques. The first technique enabled me to still my mind by watching my breath. The second technique allowed me to abide in the stillness by listening for the Om vibration. The Om vibration is the source of all creation; to listen to it is reviving and uplifting.

The pinnacle of Yogananda's instruction is the Kriya Yoga technique. This is more than a way to meditate. It is a method of breathing intended to facilitate spiritual development and free a person from the cycle of reincarnation. Life in this troubled world held no promise of joy for me, and I never wanted to be born again. With the hope of liberation from the cycle of rebirth, I prepared to receive initiation into Kriya Yoga. The qualification to receive this initiation was the consistent practice of the other techniques for at least six months. Meanwhile, by stilling my mind and abiding in the stillness, I renewed my energy and empowered myself to move forward with my life.

As I reflected on Yogananda's writings, my understanding of Jesus changed. Yogananda taught that Jesus was an embodiment of the enlightened state of consciousness he called Christ Consciousness. Jesus became for me one of many great enlightened souls rather than a unique individual sent as the savior of all mankind. I continued to attend the Methodist Church during this transition period, and initially, I was uncomfortable with my new view of Jesus. It took a year for me to be at ease with Yogananda as my chosen spiritual teacher.

I loved Yogananda's idea of the brotherhood of all religions. He declared, "We should begin to build world unity with respect for all religions as constituting various paths to God."[3] In my mind, religions had too much in common to create divisions by focusing on their differences. I embraced Yogananda's vision of respect for all faith traditions.

After reading the *Autobiography of a Yogi*, I looked for colleges in Los Angeles near the headquarters of the Self-Realization Fellowship. I found out that Occidental College was just a few miles away. I applied, and Occidental accepted me as an incoming freshman. I made plans to go to Los Angeles without ever having been to a Self-Realization Fellowship meeting or having met another follower of Yogananda. As my graduation approached, all I could think about was going to Los Angeles to progress on my spiritual journey. Within days of completing high school, I left for a summer term at Occidental College.

The highlight of the summer was a series of Self-Realization Fellowship classes. After class one night, I could not distinguish myself from the world around me. My identity merged with everything in my surroundings. I was alive in a profound sense of oneness. The promise of more such experiences kept me engaged in meditation and the study of Yogananda's lessons.

I was only in Los Angeles for a few weeks when my mother threatened to take me out of school. She thought I was being brainwashed by a cult. She told me, "You have to stop following that Indian guru or leave school and come home." I was angry. My psychotherapist in Oroville had referred me to a colleague in Beverly Hills. I talked to him about my mother's threat. He suggested she come to Los Angeles to meet with him and talk about her concerns.

I called her and said, "Mom, would you please come to Los Angeles and meet with my therapist to discuss my participation in the Self-Realization Fellowship?"

She could tell this was important to me and replied, "Yes, I will come."

Both my parents came. My mother expressed her concerns, and my therapist assured her the Self-Realization Fellowship was a legitimate organization with reputable members. She calmed down and allowed me to pursue my new religion. What a relief to have that drama behind me!

My therapist had created an intensive form of group therapy that he called marathon therapy. I participated in two eighteen-hour marathon therapy sessions for teens. We spoke openly about our difficulties, and I shared with them my reaction to my French teacher's disclosure of his sexual attraction to me. I had a new sense of freedom as a result of my self-expression.

By the end of the summer, I was unable to focus on my studies. As thrilling as those intensive therapy sessions were, they left me without healthy social boundaries. I acted like my life was an extension of therapy, often dropping my defenses and talking freely about my emotional issues and my spiritual experience of oneness. Some of the men in the dorm reported to the dean of students that I was acting like a zombie. Just before the end of the summer term, the dean called me into his office and confronted me with their comments. It was a crushing blow to find out other students thought I was weird. The dean left the door open for me to return the next term, but if I did, I knew I would have to face my reputation.

I went home for the break before the fall term and did not go back. My summer in Los Angeles overwhelmed me. I withdrew into a depressed state with fleeting suicidal thoughts. I had moved away from home to start my own life. I returned defeated. A few weeks later, I registered at Yuba College, the local community college. The structure of commuting and attending classes allowed me to refocus and cope with my stress.

I wrote to the Self-Realization Fellowship to find out if there were any other members near my home in Oroville. They referred me to a retired couple, Jesse and Berneice, who lived in the area. I contacted them, and they welcomed me into their lives. Twice a week we met in their home to meditate and pray. With them, I felt safe, appreciated, and understood. Our time together gave me peace of mind and provided an opportunity to practice the meditation techniques in a small group setting. Berneice prepared us for meditation by playing songs on the organ that Yogananda had sung. Our meetings were uplifting and spiritually nourishing.

The following spring, I accepted the invitation of one of my friends to spend the summer with Volunteers in Service to America (VISTA) as part of President Johnson's War on Poverty. For ten weeks we provided a support system for migrant farm workers living near Marysville, California, who were mostly from Mexico. We addressed their needs for housing, clothing, food, and health care by connecting them to existing community services and generating resources on their behalf. Some of my childhood playmates had been children of farm workers from Mexico who worked for my father. I had a deep appreciation for the loving kindness extended to me by one family in particular. I welcomed the chance to return their kindness by being a VISTA volunteer.

The needs of the people we served were great, and it frustrated me we couldn't do more. I put aside my frustrations and devoted myself to what we could do. One of my responsibilities was to conduct a survey to identify health care needs. I got the assignment because I spoke Spanish, thanks to some Spanish classes I had taken. As I asked the prescribed questions and recorded the responses, I felt the dedication of those people to create a better life for their families by leaving their familiar surroundings in Mexico to work in California. I was glad I could be of service.

After my summer with VISTA and a year of frequent meditations with Jesse and Berneice, I thought I might find fulfillment in a life devoted to meditation and service. To explore this option, I applied to the monastic order founded by Yogananda located in Encinitas, California. Yogananda had joined a monastery at my age, and I was considering following his example.

My mother was upset when she found out I had applied to be a monk. My therapist in Beverly Hills and I were still in touch, and again he acted as my advocate. I convinced my mother to talk with him about my application to the monastery. With his coaching, she gave up her open opposition to my interest in renouncing marriage and devoting myself to a religious community.

Several months later, the monastery responded to my application. Their guidance was simple: "Your life course is to marry and have children rather than live as a celibate monk." Their advice gave me the clarity I needed to confidently plan to one day get married and raise a family.

It was the middle of the Vietnam War, and I was subject to the draft. Acceptance in the monastery would have provided me with a military deferment when I finished my education. Rather than join the army as an enlisted man, I decided to serve my country as an officer when I graduated from college. A naval officer candidate program accepted my application, and I was on track to serve in the navy when I completed my bachelor's degree.

As I began my last semester in junior college, my sister was making wedding plans. She asked me if I would sing at her wedding, "The Lord's Prayer." To prepare, I started taking lessons again with my singing teacher, Winifred. Under her direction, I entered a singing competition at Chico State University. The song for my performance was from Handel's *Messiah*. I stood in front of the judges and sang, "Thus saith the Lord, the Lord of hosts: Yet once a little while and I will shake the heavens and the earth, the sea and the dry land. And I will shake all nations; and the desire of all nations shall come. The Lord, whom ye seek, shall suddenly come to His temple, even the messenger of the Covenant, whom ye delight in; behold, He shall come, saith the Lord of hosts."[4] As I practiced that piece over and over again, the declaration "He shall come" sank into my heart. I didn't know the timing or the significance of His coming. I only knew Jesus Christ would return.

Those three years, from 1966 to 1969, were a period of awakening. I faced depression, returned home from a failed attempt to go away to college, and found refuge in a community college near my home. I meditated with Self-Realization Fellowship friends, served as a VISTA volunteer and applied for a monastery. The navy accepted me in an officer candidate program, and I came to know Jesus would one day return. While I was having all those experiences, following Yogananda and his teachings gave me purpose and hope.

Notes:

1. Psalms 46:10.

2. Yogananda. (1946). *Autobiography of a Yogi.* Los Angeles: Self-Realization Fellowship.

3. Yogananda. https://yoganandasite.wordpress.com/2016/04/17/meaning-of-srfyss-and-church-of-all-religions/ Accessed March 13, 2018.

4. Handel, G. (1742). "Thus Saith the Lord." From the *Messiah.* New York: G. Schirmer.

CHAPTER 4

"WHY DON'T YOU GO TO BRIGHAM YOUNG UNIVERSITY?"

YOGANANDA RECOMMENDED SURROUNDING yourself with good people. He taught that your spiritual life is like a seedling that needs to be protected with good company. He declared, "Environment is stronger than willpower."[1] With his advice in mind, I looked for people who lived a committed life of faith.

In the fall term of 1968, I met several students in a folk dancing class who impressed me. I eventually found out they were all members of the Church of Jesus Christ of Latter-day Saints. When the class ended, so did our association with each other.

In the spring semester, I ran into a high-school friend, David Goddard, who was also taking classes at the college. When he told me he had just returned from serving a mission for the Church of Jesus Christ of Latter-day Saints, I decided to renew our friendship and find out what was different about Latter-day Saints. I started having lunch with David every day in the school cafeteria.

David was entirely at peace with himself. His self-assurance and calm demeanor fed my curiosity. When I asked him about his church, he referred me to two young men serving as missionaries. I met with them, and they tried to engage me in thoughtful discussions on various gospel topics. I was unwilling to reexamine what I already believed. When they told me that their church was the only church that had the fullness of the gospel, I stopped listening, and I dismissed their message as too exclusive. They seemed to be isolating themselves from other religions rather than fostering mutual respect.

During one of our lunches, I asked David what he did on weekends. I didn't know what to do with myself when I wasn't busy with school work. In my free time, I just read, meditated, or watched TV. David told me that on Saturdays, his family did things around the house. I announced I would come and help. The next Saturday, I joined his family in painting the exterior of their home. After several hours of work, we went inside for refreshments.

Mrs. Goddard couldn't bear to watch us sit at the kitchen table, totally unproductive. To make good use of our time, she gave us a bowl of walnuts to crack. Over the sound of breaking walnut shells, she asked me where I was going to school in the fall.

"I'll probably go to Chico State," I answered with a shrug. Even though I was nearly done with my two-year program, I had not given any thought to where I would go next. I needed to stay in school as part of my plan to complete a bachelor's degree and become a naval officer. Chico State seemed like just as good a place as any to get a degree.

"Why don't you go to Brigham Young University?" she asked.

I knew nothing about BYU except that David would be going there in the fall. However, if there were people like David at BYU—spiritually minded and sympathetic to a God-centered way of life—then that was where I wanted to go.

I asked, "How do I apply?"

In response, she sifted through some papers on the counter and handed me an application form.

When I told my parents that I was applying to BYU, they were glad I was moving forward with my life—they would have been just as happy if I went to Chico State. With hope for my future, I completed the application. Part of the process was to have an interview with the local church leader. I met with him, and he gave me the endorsement I needed. As I waited for a response from the university, I anticipated having the companionship of the good people I expected to meet there. By applying to BYU, I was acting on Yogananda's counsel to surround yourself with good company.

Notes:

1. Yogananda. https://howfarwillirun.com/2013/07/01/environment-is-stronger-than-will-power-paramahansa-yogananda/ Accessed April 17, 2018.

CHAPTER 5

A MIRACULOUS MEETING!

AFTER DAVID AND I finished the school year, we drove to BYU. David wanted to visit his girlfriend, and I wanted to see the campus. With some of David's friends, we toured the university. We could see the social life waiting for us as future students. Our short visit made it clear: BYU was the place for me. We met welcoming people who were at ease with their commitment to a life of faith. This was the spiritually empowering environment I was looking for.

When we returned, I was off to Europe to visit friends. I flew to Zurich and took the train to Lausanne to visit a friend, Peter, who was serving a French-speaking mission for the Church of Jesus Christ of Latter-day Saints. He had gone to BYU before his mission. Because I was headed in that direction, I was eager to see him. In Lausanne, we attended church together. After church, Peter told me he was going to share the gospel with a man who couldn't see the value of attending an indoor church meeting. He wanted to commune with God on his own outdoors. Through our brief visit and Peter's description of the man he was going to teach, I got a glimpse of what it was like to be a missionary.

I then flew from Geneva to London to see people I had met the summer I served at the Baden-Powell House. I soon discovered the Hyde Park chapel of the Church of Jesus Christ of Latter-day Saints nearby. In anticipation of going to BYU, I went inside to see who I could meet. I met Elder Robert Galbraith, who was on a special mission as the organist for the chapel's 2,000-pipe organ. I loved listening to him play. I told Elder Galbraith I was from Northern California, and he told me he was too. For the next few weeks, he and his companion attempted to teach me. I heard what they had to say, but I had no real interest. I was satisfied with my choice to follow Yogananda.

On one of my visits to the Hyde Park chapel, I met a group of young adults planning a day trip to the London temple, and I went with them. On the way, they told me the temple is a special place to provide blessings for our ancestors. They taught me more by their reverence for the temple than by their explanations of its purpose. On the temple grounds, there was an embracing atmosphere of peace and well-being. It didn't matter that I wasn't able to go inside—I found fulfillment in the companionship of those young people, and as a bonus, I discovered the temple grounds as a sacred place.

When I returned home to Oroville, I accepted an invitation to speak at a church meeting about my visit with Peter in Switzerland. This was the congregation Peter's family attended, and everyone wanted news about his mission. By that time, I had received my acceptance letter to BYU. It was an honor to have a few minutes to talk about my trip and announce I was going to BYU. I was right at home in front of those Latter-day Saints. Many of them I knew from attending meetings with them while the missionaries were attempting to teach me.

Afterward, at the invitation of Mrs. Goddard, I went to her home to have dinner and show slides of my trip. She had also invited the Hunt family, who were visiting from out of town. Over dinner, we got to know Mitch, Bette, and their four children.

Meeting the Hunts was an extraordinary experience. Bette led the way in welcoming me into their lives. When I greeted her, she said, "When I saw you sitting in front of the chapel waiting to give your talk, I thought you were a member of the bishopric." I was surprised that she thought I might be one of the three men who led the congregation. I was only twenty years old, and it gave me a sense of importance that anyone would confuse me with a church leader.

I fit right in with the Hunt children. One son, Mitchell, was a little older than I, and another son, David, was a little younger. They both showed interest in my summer trip and wanted to get to know me better. Even the youngest brother, Murray, and their sister, Rebecca, enjoyed my slides and were curious about why I was going to BYU. I loved the warmth and attention they gave me. The whole family treated me as if I was a long-lost relative.

During our conversations, they told me they knew Elder Galbraith, the missionary who taught me in London. Mitchell was good friends with Robert in high school and introduced him to the Church. Robert even met with the missionaries in the Hunts' home to study the gospel. His relationship with the Hunt family paved the way for him to become a Latter-day Saint.

This was miraculous! The family who introduced Elder Galbraith to the Church was not only visiting from out of town, but I was having dinner with them. This was not a chance meeting; it was an answer to Elder Galbraith's prayers. To add to my amazement, Bette's father had been a mission president[1] in London and had helped select the site for the London temple. In parting, the Hunts invited me to visit them in their home near San Francisco. Before I left for BYU a few weeks later, I paid them a visit.

The father, Mitch, was unlike anyone I had ever met. He was at peace with himself and intentional in everything he did. Even though he was self-disciplined, there was an ease about him. He had served as a bishop of their congregation and was now the teacher of a class for people interested in the Church. In the class, he listened to me in such a way that I felt heard. When he taught, he expressed himself with a peaceful assurance that what he said was true. I was more impressed by how he spoke than by what he said.

As we walked with one of his friends after church, Mitch explained that he had gone to Oroville to explore an investment opportunity. He was specifically looking for a way to raise money to send one of his sons on a mission. His clarity of purpose was unfamiliar to me. My father often looked at investment opportunities, but never with a particular goal in mind. Mitch had included his family in what was primarily a business trip. My father never combined business with family activities. Mitch experienced life as an integrated whole rather than as disconnected activities. He was a marvel.

I also saw this balance in his home life. He had a way of being with his family that was both powerful and nurturing. While his children and I watched TV, he sat nearby reading the newspaper. It felt like he was lovingly watching over us. His approach to parenting made me feel like I was a welcome part of their family.

The way they all related to each other gave me a new idea about what it meant to be a family. Before they bought their house, they counseled together to define what they wanted. A swimming pool was a priority for the children. Mitch agreed to buy a house with a pool if the children assumed responsibility for cleaning it. He followed through on his end of the agreement and held them to theirs. The openness of their communication and the acceptance of accountability appealed to me.

While I was there, Bette spent hours alone in the dining room absorbed in her preparations for a presentation to the Relief Society, the women's organization of the Church. As she came in and out of the dining room, she seemed both scattered and preoccupied.

Mitch and Bette were very different, yet it was clear they loved each other. Their love blended their unique personalities into a separate and distinct unit as a couple. The quality of their relationship taught me that marriage can be a place where you can be your own person and expand as part of a loving union. Their unity served as the stable center for their family. How they related to their children provided me with an example of a deeply felt family connection.

Those precious days with the Hunts exposed me to what it is like to put your family at the center of your life of faith. Even though the quality of their relationships appealed to me, it was in stark contrast to my expectations for my future family. My priority was to achieve spiritual enlightenment through meditation. For me, marriage and family were incidental to my spiritual quest. I couldn't imagine putting my family first.

Notes:

1. A mission president provides leadership and guidance for full-time missionaries for the Church of Jesus Christ of Latter-day Saints in a specific geographic area.

CHAPTER 6

THE MAGIC OF BRIGHAM YOUNG UNIVERSITY

MY SPORTS CAR was very cool. It was a rare prototype car with a roll bar and a fiberglass body. I loved the looks of amazement from people who saw me driving down the road. My car was a representation of how I saw myself—avant-garde, with flair. It set me apart from the ordinary, just as my religion set me apart.

I could barely fit everything I needed for school into my little car for the drive from California to Utah. As I crossed the Nevada desert toward BYU, surrounded by my belongings, I reflected on my life since high school. I'd come out of Yuba College with an associate's degree in liberal arts, ready for the next chapter of my life. This was my second attempt to leave home and go away to college. My heart was set on succeeding academically and progressing on my spiritual journey.

After a day of driving, I pulled up to my new home close to the mountains that loom above BYU's campus. I had rented a private room in a brick, ranch-style home owned by a BYU professor. My room offered me the solitude to meditate undisturbed and to study without distractions. Though being alone was important, I welcomed the opportunity to attend church with students in the neighborhood. As I joined them in worship, I found the fulfillment of the scriptural promise, "Where two or more are gathered together in my name, there I am in the midst of them" (Matthew 18:10). In their meetings, there was a sacred presence. What a joy to be with good people who generated a vital experience of the divine!

The Sunday School lessons gave me another exposure to the doctrines of the Church, but I filtered them through my understanding of what Yogananda taught. For example, any reference to Jesus became an acknowledgment of Him as a pioneer in manifesting the divine state of awareness Yogananda called Christ Consciousness. A reference to the Spirit became a reference to the divine Om vibration. If Yogananda was silent on a topic, such as Christ's atoning sacrifice for mankind, I gave it no importance. I enjoyed the lessons without paying attention to their intended meaning.

On the first Sunday of the semester, the church leaders passed around a survey asking us about our talents and our previous positions of leadership. My friends filled out the survey, eager to be of service. They weren't interested in acknowledgment. Their desire to serve was an expression of their faith in Christ. I decided to follow their example and provide selfless service on campus.

First, I looked for an opportunity to sing. I joined a song and dance group and went into rehearsal for a performance of a medley of George M. Cohan songs. In straw hats and red-and-white striped vests, we ran on stage singing, "Give My Regards to Broadway, Remember me to Herald Square, Tell all the gang at Forty-Second Street that I will soon be there!"[1] It was fun, but I was looking for a closer connection to people.

I noticed a flyer about the Boy Scout fraternity, Alpha Phi Omega. I went to a fraternity meeting and found just what I wanted—companionship and service opportunities. All thirty-five of us were Eagle Scouts. Among my fraternity brothers, I had an unprecedented sense of belonging. Our connection as brothers developed as we shared the joy of serving the BYU community.

Only a few weeks into the semester, Bette Hunt showed up outside my last class of the day. She wasted no time inviting me to attend General Conference, the semi-annual meeting of the Church of Jesus Christ of Latter-day Saints, in Salt Lake City. I agreed to go with her, and the following morning I sat with Bette and Mitch in the Tabernacle on

Temple Square for the opening session. I thrilled in the power and majesty of the Tabernacle Choir, the prayers, and the talks.

After the conference, we went to see Bette's father, A. Hamer Reiser. In his modest home, we had a brief conversation. I don't remember anything he said. I only remember the peace and vibrancy he radiated. He had an impressive career managing the publishing company Deseret Book, providing leadership for full-time missionaries, and working as an assistant to the president of the Church, David O. McKay. However, what really struck me was his empowering presence. His way of being made such an impression on me that my memory of our few moments together has persisted for a lifetime.

In the university environment of spiritually minded people, I was able to keep a daily regimen of meditation and prayer. This is what I had hoped for. It was the first time since I began my training with Yogananda that I consistently meditated both morning and night.

With my daily meditations came a burning in my heart. I wrote a letter to the Self-Realization Fellowship asking if they had an explanation for this strong sense of warmth in my chest. When I got a letter back suggesting I consult with a physician, I chose to ignore the feeling. I was confident there was nothing physically wrong with me.

In my quest to fellowship with the best people I could find, I attended devotionals in the Smith Fieldhouse. Every Tuesday morning more than ten thousand students packed the arena. We went to hear the most distinguished leaders of the Church impart their spiritual guidance. I could count on hearing uplifting and invigorating words of wisdom. One Tuesday morning, I was in a crowd of students on the way to our seats when we heard the announcement of the opening prayer. We stopped and bowed our heads. An embracing reverence descended upon us as we united in heart with the invocation.

On one occasion, Joseph Fielding Smith, the president of the Church, came to speak. Before he spoke, his wife, Jessie Evans Smith, sang. She had been an accomplished soloist in her younger years. Sister Smith sang with great feeling, "Let There Be Peace on Earth."[2] What an extraordinary appeal to God in song! She sang as if she knew Heavenly Father rejoiced in hearing her sing. That declaration of her commitment to peace on earth lingered in my heart.

In those devotionals, I heard most of the highest-level leaders of the Church speak on a wide range of gospel topics. At some point in their talks, they each shared their testimony of the gospel and Jesus Christ. I was able to rejoice with them in their testimonies while remaining apart. Though I had vivid, enduring impressions of their declarations that Jesus is the Christ and the gospel is true, I did not think their message was for me.

All the students at BYU took two Book of Mormon classes. Latter-day Saints believe the book is a testament to Jesus Christ and a record of the relationship between God and people who lived in ancient America. They also profess that the prophet, Mormon, compiled it in the fourth century, and Joseph Smith translated the book into English by the gift and power of God. The impact of those two courses on me was greater than any other classes I took in my entire college career.

As a transferring junior, I was able to take an upper division Book of Mormon class entitled "A Doctrinal Approach to the Book of Mormon." The professor, Glenn L. Pearson, taught with authority and power. Time and again, I marveled at how he had distilled the essence of the gospel into such pithy statements of truth. He impressed me as an extraordinarily gifted teacher.

His instruction was both intellectual and inspirational. In one class, Brother[3] Pearson explained that in every philosophical system there is a moral imperative, or a way to know if something is good. He said, "For a Christian, the moral imperative is—what leads to Christ is good, and what does not lead to Christ is not good." I loved the simplicity of this standard for discerning goodness. He also taught the importance of being "founded on the rock." He asserted that we are responsible for establishing our lives on the rock which is Jesus Christ. Brother Pearson's boldness and faith inspired me.

The concept of a "broken heart" (3 Nephi 9:20, Book of Mormon) was new to me. Brother Pearson explained that to have a broken heart is to be receptive to the guidance of Jesus Christ. The promised blessings of following Him with a broken heart are inner peace and freedom. He warned us not to confuse a broken heart with a broken spirit. He explained, "While a broken heart empowers us in our relationship with Christ, a broken spirit cuts us off from Him and leaves us in despair."

His warning drew my attention. I wanted to have inner peace and freedom, but despite my efforts, these qualities eluded me. Clearly, my spirit was broken, and I was not fully available to God. My personal trials were daunting my spirit and preventing me from being completely free and at peace. Even with this insight, I was unmoved. I thought all I had to do was meditate. I was confident my meditations would eventually resolve my internal conflicts and provide me with a profound awareness of oneness with God.

I went to BYU committed to my existing ideas and viewpoints. My boyhood love for Scouting was the basis for my connection to my fraternity brothers, and my religious views gave me the frame of reference for relating to the gospel. As much as I enjoyed Brother Pearson's guidance and the testimonies of the leaders of the Church, I fit what I heard into what I already knew.

Notes:

1. Cohan, G. (1904). "Give My Regards to Broadway." New York: F. A. Mills.

2. Jackson-Miller, J., & Miller, S. (1955). "Let there be Peace on Earth." Penn Valley, California: Jan-Lee Music.

3. We referred to all the professors at BYU as either Brother or Sister followed by their last name regardless of their academic accomplishments.

CHAPTER 7

THE WONDERS OF REVELATION

THE USUAL ROLL call proceeded on the first day of my Book of Mormon class in the spring semester of 1970: "Bingham ... Booth ... Bowers."

"Here," I answered.

"Are you Donna?" asked Brother Pearson with a smile. A few rows over, the real Donna Bowers raised her hand. After class, Donna shared a laugh with me over my confusion. In our short conversation, we discovered we had a lot in common, and we soon became close friends.

Donna was very religious, just as I was. She had served as a full-time missionary for eighteen months for the Church of Jesus Christ of Latter-day Saints and continued to live her faith wholeheartedly. The devotion to God we shared was the basis for our friendship. On Sundays, sometimes I attended her church meetings. As part of our religious practices, we both fasted at least once a month. She fasted without food or water, and I drank only orange juice, following Yogananda's recommendation. Donna's devotional activities included going to the Salt Lake City temple every week. When she returned, she glowed. I didn't know what she did in the temple, but I knew it drew her closer to God.

In our friendship, we had ease and freedom. We were both committed to marrying someone of our own faith, and as a result, we were close friends without becoming boyfriend and girlfriend. I met her family in Salt Lake City, we went to movies together, and we took drives in the countryside. She respected me for my commitment to follow Yogananda's guidance to fast, meditate, and put God first in my life. I never had a sense she was trying to get me to accept the gospel. She freely extended her unconditional love and acceptance.

More than two years after our first meeting, Donna and I were sitting together on campus having a conversation. At one point, she became serious.

"Tom, someday you are going to join the Church." I could tell her statement came on the foundation of prayer and fasting.

I said, "That's unlikely," though I did not dismiss it as impossible.

She added, "I'm getting married."

This came as a surprise. She wasn't dating anyone, and I asked, "Who are you going to marry?"

She answered, "I haven't met him yet, but the Lord told me I will soon." That was the Donna I knew—a woman who received and trusted revelation.

The Lord fulfilled His promise a few months later. She met Terry Harding in the Salt Lake City temple and married him the following spring. The fulfillment of her marriage revelation added credibility to her declaration that I would join the Church. I kept in my heart her prophetic words that one day I would be a Latter-day Saint.

In his Book of Mormon course, Brother Pearson challenged us with the question, "How do you know something is true?" As he explained epistemology, or the theory of knowledge, I listened attentively. He said, "All knowledge is obtained in one of four ways: the physical senses, reason, authority, or revelation."

He proceeded to explain in detail the first three ways of knowing. Then Brother Pearson turned the discussion to the fourth way of knowing—revelation.

He asserted, "Of all the ways of knowing, revelation carries with it the strongest sense of certainty that something is true. Revelation can be so vivid that you can't deny it."

He continued, "At the age of fourteen, Joseph Smith saw Heavenly Father and Jesus Christ. He recounted in later years, 'Though I was hated and persecuted for saying that I had seen a vision, yet it was true ... I knew it, and I knew that God knew it, and I could not deny it, neither dared I do it.'"[1] Brother Pearson further explained, "Joseph Smith's statement—'I knew it, and God knew that I knew it'—reveals one of the characteristics of revelation. A person who receives a revelation often knows that God knows he has received one."

Brother Pearson added, "The Holy Spirit is the instrument of revelation." He then referenced John 14:26: "But the Comforter, which is the Holy Ghost, whom the Father will send in my name, He shall teach you all things, and bring all things to your remembrance, whatsoever I have said unto you." He expounded on this verse by saying, "When the Holy Spirit teaches us or brings things to our remembrance, He adds His own witness to what He reveals."

In his description of the ways of knowing, Brother Pearson included an explanation of the principle of reproducibility. He proclaimed, "Just as scientific results are reliably reproducible, anyone can know if the gospel is true." He expanded the scope of science, usually the domain of the five senses, to include revelation by applying the principle of reproducibility.

Yogananda had written a book called *The Science of Religion*.[2] From his book, the idea that religion and science could inform each other was familiar to me. However, the principle of reproducibility had not occurred to me as a link between science and religion.

Brother Pearson connected this principle to a passage in the Book of Mormon that provides the formula for verifying its truthfulness. In that verse, the prophet Mormon's son, Moroni, promises, "If ye shall ask with a sincere heart, with real intent, having faith in Christ, he will manifest the truth of it unto you, by the power of the Holy Ghost" (Moroni 10:4). With a quiet, authoritative declaration, Brother Pearson testified that he had seen many people apply this formula, and it had never failed.

I believed Brother Pearson, and I was confident that if anyone followed these instructions, the predicted confirmation of the Book of Mormon's truthfulness would follow. However,

I was not curious. I was content to know the application of the formula would result in knowing the Book of Mormon was true without any interest in knowing for myself.

I was confident I knew what he was talking about. Yogananda taught that when someone knows something spiritually, he knows he knows.[3] I was certain that all I needed to do was to continue what I was already doing, and I would come to know that I knew. I persisted in my daily meditations in my quest to know God.

Donna wasn't the only friend I had at BYU who dynamically lived their faith. My fraternity brothers did so as well. When an opening came in the fall of 1970 to share an apartment with some of them, I gave up the privacy of my single room and moved in. All three of my roommates had served for two years as full-time missionaries and were active Latter-day Saints.

As roommates, we took turns grocery shopping and cooking. When I cooked, I made vegetarian meals. I introduced them to soy hotdogs and my specialty, cottage cheese casserole. They accepted whatever I made in a spirit of discovery.

My roommate, Michael, sometimes came home late after spending the evening with his fiancée, Tara. Occasionally when he came in, he would find me in the corner of our room engrossed in meditation. Other times, when I came home late, Michael would be on his knees at the side of his bed—sound asleep. No matter how tired he was when he came home, he knelt in prayer before going to bed. My roommates respected my religious practices, and I respected theirs.

One day, while sitting with Michael in our apartment, I asked if he had any opinion about Joseph Smith's claim that Heavenly Father and Jesus Christ live on another planet. It hit me, as Michael responded, that he was not speculating. What he told me was real for him. For me, his church's ideas were theoretical. Michael gave me a glimpse of what it meant to *know* the gospel is true. His assurance in what he believed moved me.

Our conversation got me thinking about what it meant for my friends when they said they had a testimony. In church meetings, I heard my friends and other students share what they knew to be true. They expressed their faith with conviction and emotion. For example, they often made one of the following statements: "I know that Jesus is the Christ and Joseph Smith is a prophet of God." "I know that the Church of Jesus Christ of Latter-day Saints is the one true church on the earth." "I know that through the authority of the priesthood, families can be bound together forever." "I know I am a child of God and He loves me." Initially, I didn't see the connection between these expressions of belief and their lives.

Michael's explanation of what he believed allowed me to see that a testimony serves as a frame of reference for Latter-day Saints. Their testimonies of the workings of the Spirit and doctrines of the Church are woven together to create the fabric of their lives, and what they do is intended to be an expression of what they *know* to be true.

At one point, I felt my roommates were praying I would accept their religion. They authentically cared about me. They valued their faith and hoped I would accept it for myself. However, they made no external attempts to get me to join.

In my last semester as an undergraduate in the spring of 1971, I had no career plans. To explore my options, I went to the counseling office and took an interest test. The results suggested I would enjoy being a librarian. I could not see myself as a librarian and dismissed the test's findings. Instead, I chose to stay at the university and continue my study of sociology in a master's degree program. For the next two years, I continued to have positive experiences at BYU, surrounded by people who loved and served God. All the while, I maintained my commitment to Yogananda and the Self-Realization Fellowship.

In graduate school, Duane was my closest friend. We met in a psychology class in the fall of 1971. He had an inner peace I admired. One Sunday not long after we met, I attended a church meeting with him. He, as one of the bishop's counselors, sat in the front of the room, and I sat in the congregation.

The most important and sacred part of the Sunday meetings of the Church of Jesus Christ of Latter-day Saints is remembering the Lord by taking bread and water as symbols of his body and blood. In preparation for the blessing and passing of the bread and water that day, we sang "I Stand All Amazed."[4] When we expressed in song the wonder of the Lord's grace, my eyes filled with tears as love washed over me. The song and the uplifting atmosphere broke through my conceptual filters and opened my heart. Any time I reflect back on singing that hymn, I know I'm loved.

Pursuing my master's degree gave me an opportunity to become friends with a group of research assistants with whom I shared an office. After working side by side for almost a year, they finally convinced me to fast and pray with them to know if the message of the Church of Jesus Christ of Latter-day Saints was true. Somehow, my commitment to follow Yogananda did not discourage them from reaching out to me. I felt their genuine concern and decided to appease them.

Six months after I felt God's love in the church meeting with Duane, I made my best attempt to pray to know if the gospel was true. During our fast, we traveled to a golf course and prayed together just before dark. It was a good place to open our hearts to God. After a representative prayer, we separated for private prayer. When we reassembled, they asked me if I had received an answer. I said, "Yes, I received a decisive answer. God told me, 'If you want to know, I will tell you.'" I added, "The choice is easy—I don't want to know."

My response surprised them, but they didn't hassle me. I was committed to the course that I had already set for myself, and I rejected the divine offer to know if the gospel was true.

Notes:

1. Smith, J. "Joseph Smith History." In *The Pearl of Great Price*. Salt Lake City, Utah: Church of Jesus Christ of Latter-Day Saints, 1989.

2. Yogananda. (1953). *The Science of Religion*. Los Angeles: Self-Realization Fellowship.

3. Yogananda. (1974). "He Who Knows." In *Cosmic Chants*. Los Angeles: Self-Realization Fellowship.

4. Gabriel, C. (1898). "I Stand All Amazed." In *Hymns of The Church of Jesus Christ of Latter-day Saints*, 1985. Salt Lake City, Utah: The Church of Jesus Christ of Latter-day Saints.

Chapter 8

A Minority of One

When I went to BYU in 1969, there were 25,000 students. At the beginning of the school year, one thousand of us were not members of the Church of Jesus Christ of Latter-day Saints. After one semester, there were only five hundred of us left who had not joined the Church. Most of the non-member students converted by the time they graduated. Within the small minority of students who did not become Latter-day Saints, I was the only one who was a member of the Self-Realization Fellowship. I was a minority of one.

My friends used to tease me, "You are an *instant* member. All we have to do is add water." I looked like a prime candidate for baptism. As a student at BYU, I kept the honor code, which included abstinence from tobacco, alcohol, coffee, and tea, as well as chastity before marriage. With converting me on their minds, sometimes students befriended me only to drop out of my life when I didn't progress toward baptism. I initially took offense. Over time, I got used to it.

Occasionally, someone would ask me if I had served a mission for the Church. I considered their question a compliment. On campus, I often saw missionaries from the training center. They had something I didn't have. I envied them. I aspired to emanate goodness and purity as they did. My desire to be like them drove me to meditate and study Yogananda's teachings with greater zeal.

While I was at BYU, there was negative press regarding the Church. Boycotts put a dark cloud over BYU athletics. People thought it was racist to deny the priesthood to black men. In my Book of Mormon class, Brother Pearson addressed the issue. He assured us that the Lord would grant the priesthood to black men in His own due time, not in response to public pressure. His counsel inspired confidence in me that the priesthood is intended for all men. In my opinion, representatives of the media were not willing to get behind the scenes and understand the hearts and minds of the leaders of the Church. A few years later, Brother Pearson's prediction came true. Through a revelation from the Lord and the leadership of the president of the Church, the priesthood became available to all men.

While I was home on school breaks, I often spoke out in favor of the Church. Not everyone shared my positive attitude. Some people opposed the Church without much exposure to it. My father was a typical example. He had been in a failed business transaction with some Latter-day Saints, and he generalized his bitterness toward them to the entire church. In his mind, he knew what members of the Church were like from personal experience.

I had a different perspective. Among Latter-day Saints, I saw a broad spectrum of responses to the challenge of gospel living. In my mind, the only way to judge the Church was by the lives of members who practiced what they believed. The faithful members I observed never ceased to amaze me. No matter what came their way, they rose to the occasion and benefited from the difficulties they faced.

As I worshipped with them, listened attentively to their leaders, and studied their teachings, I was confident I did not know what it was to be a Latter-day Saint. Something about their way of being was out of my reach. Yogananda taught that you can describe the taste of an orange, and you can know a lot about an orange, but you can never know what it's like to taste an orange until you do. As much as I knew about Latter-day Saints, I could see they had something I had not tasted.

To me, prayer is at the heart of being a Latter-day Saint. In my senior year at BYU, I chose prayer as a topic for a term paper. I read whatever I could find on what prayer meant to

Latter-day Saints. A song in their hymnal declares, "Prayer is the soul's sincere desire, uttered or unexpressed."[1] I realized that even the desires of our hearts can serve as a prayer. I also learned what it was like to hear Brigham Young pray. One of the presidents of the Church, Heber J. Grant, relates that when he was a boy, he was often in Brigham Young's home and heard him pray. President Grant said that Brigham Young spoke "to the Lord as one man would talk to another."[2] I put these two insights together and concluded that prayer for Latter-day Saints tends to be a conversational expression of the soul's sincere desire.

Sometimes students and faculty members asked, "Why did you decide on BYU?" They assumed it was because of some academic opportunity unique to BYU. Many times, I explained that I went to BYU to find spiritual companionship and a supportive environment where I could practice my religion, but it rarely sank in. Only a few of my closest friends understood my spiritual journey had precedence over my academic pursuit.

Because I looked like a member of the Church, people often expressed surprise when I told them I wasn't. They asked, "Why not?" After I explained I was a member of the Self-Realization Fellowship, they asked what I believed. I would then share my beliefs with them, and they would share theirs with me. I loved the affinity we generated in those conversations as we connected at the level of our core convictions.

As much as I tried to fit in, there were things specific to BYU culture I did not fully grasp. Service is one example. The enthusiastic response to opportunities to serve amazed me. Many of my fraternity brothers were married, had jobs, attended school full time, and had responsibilities at Church. I marveled at how busy they were, and they were still ready for more. I didn't have nearly as much to do, and I wasn't interested in additional opportunities to serve.

In the spring of my senior year, the university had a day of service. I looked at what I had to accomplish and decided not to participate. My fraternity brothers, with all they had going on in their lives, leaped at the opportunity to pitch in. They surprised me. My friends gave their time in service that day with freedom and joy in the face of their many obligations.

The importance of marriage is something else I didn't understand. We sometimes joked that women came to BYU to get their MRS degree. In practice, it was no joke. Pairing up in preparation for marriage was an ever-present reality. By the time I was a senior, many of my fraternity brothers had wives and fiancées. I planned to marry a Self-Realizationist, but I wasn't in a hurry.

In my first semester, I met Jeannette in a Spanish course. We went out together and on group dates from time to time for about a year. Then, as a gesture of affection, I gave Jeannette my fraternity pin. For her, this was an expression of commitment. I didn't realize she thought I would consider marrying outside my faith. When Jeannette and I graduated in 1971, she hoped we would get married. It never crossed my mind. Her sister had to pull me aside and tell me what was going on. Without realizing it, I had broken Jeannette's heart.

My time at BYU remains in my memory as magical. Just as I had hoped, the faith-based environment empowered me to fully engage in my religious practices. But I got much more than a supportive environment. As I attended church meetings with Latter-day Saints, performed service with my fraternity brothers, and spoke with other students about our respective beliefs, I found fulfilling companionship and a lasting connection to people who cared about me. BYU was more than I had hoped for, and I loved it.

Notes:

1. Montgomery, J. (1818). "Prayer Is the Soul's Sincere Desire." In *Hymns of The Church of Jesus Christ of Latter-day Saints*, 1985. Salt Lake City, Utah: The Church of Jesus Christ of Latter-day Saints.

2. "Chapter 19: Earnest, Honest, Sincere Prayer." (2011). *Teachings of Presidents of the Church: Heber J. Grant*. Salt Lake City, Utah: Church of Jesus Christ of Latter-day Saints.

CHAPTER 9

A MEDITATION GROUP IN UTAH!

MY FIRST CHRISTMAS break at BYU, I went home to visit my family, who had moved to Santa Cruz. While I was in California, I drove to Sacramento to be with my Self-Realization Fellowship friends, Jesse and Berneice. Together, we had a four-hour Christmas meditation. One week later, Berneice died from a stroke. I felt her passing was divinely timed so I could attend her funeral. At the service, they played a recording of the songs she had played on the organ during our meditations together. Hearing her familiar music touched me. Overcome with the memory of her love, I wept deeply. By making this meaningful connection to Berneice, I increased my devotion to Yogananda.

I set my heart on receiving initiation into Kriya Yoga, Yogananda's highest meditation technique. I had been following Yogananda for three years, and in the supportive atmosphere of BYU, I finally succeeded in maintaining the daily practice of the preliminary techniques to qualify for Kriya Yoga initiation. In the spring of 1970, I flew to Phoenix, Arizona, received the technique, and confirmed my identity as a Self-Realizationist.

Two of Yogananda's principal followers had a background with the Church of Jesus Christ of Latter-day Saints. One of them, Laurie Pratt, was a granddaughter of an apostle of the Church, Orson Pratt. She served as an editor for Yogananda when he wrote his autobiography. The other was Faye Wright. She met Yogananda in Salt Lake City in 1931 when she was a young Latter-day Saint. While I was a member of the Self-

Realization Fellowship, she was the leader of the organization. When I met her, she moved me by her warmth and compassion. Laurie Pratt and Faye Wright's devotion to Yogananda served as an example for me.

I spent most of the summer of 1970 in training to be a naval officer in Newport, Rhode Island. The Vietnam War was winding down, and they didn't need as many officers. The navy gave the participants in the program the choice to leave at the end of the summer. I withdrew from the program and took my chances with the draft lottery. After returning home, I traveled to Encinitas, California and stayed at a Self-Realization Fellowship retreat center to renew my spirit in prayer and meditation. The intensive training at the Naval Officer Candidate School left me drained. The retreat was just what I needed to regain my spiritual vitality.

Back at BYU, I attempted to start a meditation group. I set a date, scheduled a room in the student center, and asked the Self-Realization Fellowship to send invitations to their contact list. When the time came, I waited in vain. No one came to my meeting.

The following summer, I attended a week-long series of Self-Realization Fellowship classes in Los Angeles. It was great! I was able to be with Jesse, meet other Self-Realizationists, and participate with them in the classes. I returned to BYU as a graduate student in September 1971 determined to establish a meditation group in Salt Lake City. I followed the same steps I had taken the year before: I set a date, found a location, and had the Self-Realization Fellowship send out invitations. This time it worked! Five people came. At the meeting, a couple offered their home in Sandy as a place to hold our meetings. Sandy was a perfect location. I lived in Orem, just thirty minutes away.

By the end of 1971, our small group was meeting on Friday nights and Sunday mornings for meditation, singing, and prayer. As I led the meditations, we began with a selection from Yogananda's *Cosmic Chants*. I played a small hand-pumped reed organ, and we joined in song. One of my favorite refrains was "I am He, I am He; blessed Spirit, I am He."[1] We sang those words over and over, progressively quieter until we stopped and spent several minutes sitting in the empowering spiritual presence generated by our song. To have a meditation group in Utah was the fulfillment of a dream. I loved being the catalyst to bring people together, getting to know other Self-Realizationists, and becoming part of their lives.

A year later, in the fall of 1972, my friend, Donna Bowers, accepted Terry Harding's proposal of marriage. At that point, she said, "Tom, now that I am engaged, I am going to devote myself to my fiancé. We can no longer be the close friends we have been." The loss of her companionship left a void in my life. I decided it was time to look for someone to share my future with.

I looked for a partner who was a Self-Realizationist. Robin was the obvious choice. She often attended meditation group meetings. I asked her out, and we had a great time. As we got to know each other, it seemed like we would be compatible. The key point was that Robin was also a follower of Yogananda. Satisfied we would have a fulfilling life together, I proposed marriage, and she accepted. Our wedding was in June 1973. Our union served as the fulfillment of my plan to marry within my faith.

After our wedding, Robin and I moved into an apartment near BYU while I finished my master's thesis. My roots were in California, and I wanted to return and start our life there. Robin agreed to create our life together in California. With my degree complete, we packed everything into a truck and made the move in August.

Notes:

1. Yogananda. (1974). "No Birth, No Death." In *Cosmic Chants*. Los Angeles: Self-Realization Fellowship.

CHAPTER 10

MISSING BYU

WHEN WE ARRIVED in California, we stayed with my parents while I looked for work. I started my job search without knowing what I was looking for. I hadn't given much thought to getting a job. I had devoted myself to my religious practice and my schoolwork. I discovered there were no jobs that specifically required a master's degree in sociology.

One of my father's friends managed a life insurance office in Menlo Park. Life insurance sales was not something that I had ever considered. I met with my father's friend, and his depiction of the work intrigued me. On the spot, he offered me a job. After our meeting, I prayed for guidance. I finished the prayer inspired by the possibility of empowering people around their finances. Confident in the value of the service I would provide, I signed a contract with the Connecticut General Life Insurance Company. Robin soon found office work nearby.

Connecticut General focused on marketing insurance to business owners to fund estate settlement costs. Before long, I sat down with my father to create an estate plan. I attentively listened to him and learned about his investments. In the process, I gained a new respect for him as a businessman. This was a breakthrough for me. It was the first time I had taken an interest in his point of view. Until then, I had kept him at a distance because he was often under the influence of alcohol and sometimes irritable.

With the help of a well-qualified lawyer, my parents rewrote their wills and put in place a strategy to eventually transfer their assets to their heirs. With another attorney who specialized in corporate law, we incorporated their quarry business and set up a buy/sell agreement for it. As a result of these changes, I made a significant contribution to the financial future of my family.

Shortly after I started working with Connecticut General, I took Robin to visit Bette Hunt. Since Bette and I had met in 1969, her husband had died, her children had left home, and she was living alone. I visited her to recapture some of the magic moments we had shared. Bette invited us to join her at church. I convinced Robin to go with me. We only went once. Robin did not want to go again. Growing up in Salt Lake City, in the shadow of the dominant influence of the Church of Jesus Christ of Latter-day Saints, had left her with a bias against it. It was the only time I attended church with Bette. I did not want to go without Robin.

I missed the atmosphere created at BYU by people who expressed their love for God as they lived and worked together. I wanted to be part of a similar faith-based community. Occasionally Robin and I met with Self-Realizationist friends to talk about creating a spiritual community based on Yogananda's life and work. Nothing came of our conversations. My preference was to join an existing community rather than create something of our own.

I visited a spiritual community started by Swami Kriyananda, one of Yogananda's followers in Nevada County, California. While I was there, I looked for some indication it was a place for me. I found nothing to suggest it was.

In the fall of 1974, a little more than a year after our marriage, Robin and I came to a turning point. Her mother and one of her grandmothers died of cancer in close succession. Both were dear to her, and she had drawn strength from their prayerful, loving support. She was anxious for weeks. I suggested she might find comfort in counseling. She was willing to see a therapist, and she found one who was a good fit for her. In hopes of strengthening our marriage, I also started seeing a therapist.

Rather than drawing us together, therapy resulted in our separation a few months later. As Robin's therapy progressed, she told me she was no longer interested in the Self-Realization Fellowship. My commitment to the Self-Realization Fellowship also waned. As I processed my past in therapy, I was not able to calm my mind to meditate. The primary connection between Robin and me had been our shared commitment to Yogananda. As a result of therapy, we lost that connection.

Before our marriage, Robin and I had spoken about having children. I wanted children, and she did not. I married her, confident she would change her mind. In therapy, Robin gained the freedom to express her resolve to remain childless, and I realized parenthood was not in our future as a couple. Without a common bond to Yogananda and without the hope of children, we had very little keeping us together.

In the summer of 1975, Robin and I both received tragic news. In unrelated circumstances, Robin's uncle and my brother Dan committed suicide in the same week. In the aftermath of their deaths, I was unable to be of any support to Robin. The impact of my brother's death overwhelmed me.

For years I had seen him go from one difficulty to the next, and I had anguished over his troubles. My grief over his death triggered a sense that I had failed him as his older brother, and I became suicidal. With the support of my therapist, I was able to work through my self-recrimination and my sense of the futility of life. However, for weeks, if anyone asked me how I was, I said, "I want to die, but killing myself is a bad idea." After a few months of depression, I was able to face my brother's death and affirm my life.

At the end of 1975, Robin and I agreed to a divorce. At that point, I was near the end of my contract with Connecticut General, and I was living with a roommate in Palo Alto. It was time for a change.

While I was in therapy, I put my life of faith on hold. For over a year I hardly ever prayed, meditated, or read anything spiritually empowering. To reconnect to my life of faith, I sat in front of my stereo and gave my full attention to Handel's *Messiah*. The powerful music and uplifting words inspired me. After listening to that sacred oratorio several times, I revived spiritually, and I resumed regular meditation.

I even considered reapplying to the Self-Realization Fellowship monastery to live the life of a celibate monk. I asked one of my friends who had been a Self-Realization Fellowship monk if it would be a good place for me. He told me I was going through too much personal stress to take on the discipline of that monastic tradition. I knew he was right.

Shortly after this realization, I was walking down University Avenue in Palo Alto. A young woman standing beside an easel on the sidewalk caught my attention. On the easel was a picture of a farm project. I stopped to hear what she had to say. Based on my interest, she invited me to a bus parked nearby where some of her friends told me about the Creative Community Project. It included a farm in Mendocino County where they held weekend workshops for people interested in the Unification Church. I wanted to learn more about their communal lifestyle, and I signed up to go with them to their farm.

When I got home, I told my roommate I was going to go to a workshop in the countryside. He warned me not to go and showed me a negative newspaper article about the Unification Church. He told me that when they got me to their farm, they would prevent me from leaving. His comments took the wind out of my sails. I was torn. Should I go or not? After a few minutes of soul-searching, I chose to go, but I would not go with them on their bus. In consideration of my roommate's concerns, I planned to take my car so that I could come and go as I pleased.

At the appointed time, on Friday, March 5, 1976, I met with the Unification Church members waiting on the bus. We sang songs as more people arrived. I loved the singing. One of the songs was "Edelweiss"[1] from *The Sound of Music*. My heart melted, and my fears vanished. I left my car behind and enthusiastically joined in the singing as we rode the bus to the farm.

The newspaper report that my roommate showed me may have represented someone else's experience, but it did not reflect mine. I had a wonderful weekend. I loved the sense of community, the singing, the small group meetings, and the lectures. There were over three hundred men and women at the workshop, most of them in their early twenties. I loved the energy and enthusiasm. Was this the faith-based community I was looking for?

On Sunday evening, I took the time to go to the top of a nearby hill. There, I put myself in God's hands and asked, "Shall I stay and become part of these people, or shall I leave and pick up the pieces of my life?" My contract with Connecticut General had ended a few days earlier, and I had no marital obligations. I was completely free to make a new beginning. As I quieted my mind, my answer came: "Stay!" With clarity and commitment, I came down from the hilltop and rejoined the workshop activities.

In one weekend, I redirected my life of faith from the Self-Realization Fellowship to the Unification Church. My failed marriage, my brother's death, my suicidal thoughts, and my experience in the working world had left me ready for something different. The vital communal life of faith available to me with the Unification Church captivated me. I had found the community of believers I was looking for—people who were both embracing and passionate about their beliefs.

Notes:

1. Rogers, R., & Hammerstein, O. (1960). "Edelweiss." From *The Sound of Music*. New York: Hal Leonard.

CHAPTER 11

A LIFE FILLED WITH SONG

I STAYED AT the Boonville farm for a twenty-one-day workshop and had the time of my life. It was nonstop singing, lectures, sharing, and service. Singing set the tone. We sang folk songs, popular songs, sacred songs, and songs we wrote ourselves. The first day, I awoke to the sound of someone singing. From then on, I was up early singing wake-up songs. We sang before meals, we sang before lectures, and we had a longer period of singing before the evening lectures. It was a little bit of heaven!

Six days a week we had lectures based on the *Divine Principle*[1] written by Reverend Sun Myung Moon. The instructors expressed the ideas powerfully. The first discourse was on the creation and our relationship with God as His children. There was also a lecture on how mankind fell away from God and several lectures on the process of returning to Him.

From listening to and singing Handel's *Messiah*, I was expecting Jesus Christ to return. The lectures provided a compelling argument that Reverend Moon was the promised messiah. I accepted the reasoning and concluded he was.

After my training in Boonville, I worked in Berkeley as a full-time member of what was known as the Oakland Family of the Unification Church. For the next three years, I lived in an old fraternity house on Hearst Street, across from the University of California at Berkeley. We actively engaged in group activities day and night.

The men and women had separate sleeping quarters, but otherwise we lived our lives communally. As brothers and sisters, we ate, worked, prayed, and studied together. We were in a period of preparation for marriage. In anticipation that Reverend Moon would select our spouses, we remained sexually abstinent.

My first year in the Oakland Family was a period of transition from Yogananda to Reverend Moon. It was a big change to go from quiet personal meditation morning and night to nonstop group activities. As I adapted to my new life, I felt Yogananda encouraging me to continue. In September 1976, we had just returned from a cross-country trip to hear Reverend Moon speak at the Washington Monument. Depleted from the week-long bus trip, I walked out of the Hearst Street house with the intention of leaving the Unification Church. I doubted that it was what I wanted in a life of faith. A few blocks from the church center, I saw in a storefront window a poster advertising Self-Realization Fellowship classes with a familiar picture of Yogananda. I stood for a moment looking at his picture. The following words came into my mind: "Go back." I returned to the center and joined the activities of the day.

With those two words, I was confident the Unification Church was the path for me. I wrote to the Self-Realization Fellowship and asked them to release me from my pledge to practice Yogananda's meditation techniques, and I received a response granting my request. On my first anniversary of joining the Unification Church, I created a ceremony in which I told Heavenly Father I was transferring my spiritual lineage from Yogananda to Reverend Moon. I pledged to wholeheartedly devote myself to the cause of bringing glory to God and peace on earth under Reverend Moon's guidance.

Sometimes the challenge of nonstop group activities was too much for me. I withdrew into a defensive state, lost my sense of purpose, and became discouraged. Fortunately, my leaders were able to see when I needed a change of pace, and they sent me to the workshop to reconnect with our purpose. After spending a week or two at the workshop, I would return to the center in Berkeley revived, empowered, and ready to work. Those times of renewal at the workshop were just what I needed to keep going.

Our days began and ended in prayer. Morning and night, after an opening hymn, we stood and prayed. We stood to stay awake and alert. We simultaneously voiced our prayers at a normal speaking volume or louder. With our eyes open or closed, with our heads bowed or lifted heavenward, we poured out the desires of our hearts to God. Praying together with my brothers and sisters in faith invigorated me. Hearing their heartfelt prayers empowered my own.

When I joined the Oakland Family, the International Exchange Maintenance Company was a thriving carpet cleaning business. Two of the men in the Oakland Family started the business by finding work mopping and waxing floors. For three years, I spent most of my time working with this company, cleaning carpets and selling carpet cleaning.

We worked in shifts seven days a week, twenty-four hours a day. On the night and weekend shifts, we cleaned restaurants, offices, and clothing stores. Our weekend cleaning schedule was almost nonstop. We started on Friday evening, and we went from one job to the next until Monday morning, grabbing a few hours of sleep whenever we could. On the day shifts during the week, we cleaned mostly homes. Initially, I didn't connect the work of cleaning carpets to my purpose of building the kingdom of heaven on earth. Over time, raising money by cleaning carpets became my way to contribute to saving the world. I came to love the teamwork and the challenge of pushing beyond my limits to accomplish our goals.

One day, after a night of carpet cleaning, I awoke and saw the red terracotta tiles on the roof of the old fraternity house against the blue sky. They reminded me of the tiles on the roof of my grandfather Appelbe's home in Santa Clara. Things started falling into place. He had lived in Berkeley, and he had owned a sorority house a few blocks from where I lived on Hearst Street. The white stucco exterior, the interior paneling, and the floor plan of the church center were the same as his home. It dawned on me that he had used that old fraternity house as the model for the house he built in Santa Clara! From that time on, living in the Berkeley center connected me to memories of treasured moments with my grandfather.

As a crew boss, I trained new people how to clean carpets. One of the new people who worked with me was a doctor. He had just finished medical school, and he was preparing for his residency as a pediatrician. As a result of attending our workshops, he gained a new vision for his career. Another one of my trainees was a young lawyer. She was a natural. I only had to tell her what to do once, and she got it. It was great to see capable, educated, young people share my hope for one world under God.

Many of the new members did not have a foundation of discipline in their lives and did not have much education. The ones who stayed and accepted Reverend Moon's training developed into men and women of character and often went on to complete college degrees. I saw young people without a sense of purpose come to our workshops and gain hope for themselves and the world. Their facial expressions changed from skepticism and indifference to openness and clarity of purpose. To see their determination to live their lives for the sake of others affirmed the value of our message.

In addition to carpet cleaning, I raised money by going door-to-door with cut flowers, candy, or small framed pictures. We formed teams and went out in vans. Alone or with another team member, we worked in a designated area for a couple of hours at a time before moving on. We continued in this way for ten to twelve hours a day.

We raised funds primarily to pay for the expenses of running our centers and workshops. When we could, we sent money to support various projects initiated by Reverend Moon. At times, the media expressed suspicion about where the funds were going. This was never my concern. I raised money as an offering to God. I trusted in Him that the money would be used for a wise purpose.

In December 1978, I was going from office to office in San Francisco selling framed aluminum foil prints. In one office there was a familiar spiritual presence. I noticed the name of the company above the receptionist's desk: Utah International. Those few moments in the foyer of Utah International brought a flood of feelings that reminded me of what it had been like for me at Brigham Young University. There was an atmosphere of reverence, peace, and spiritual vitality. I didn't meet anyone other than the receptionist, but what I felt was evidence to me that faithful members of the Church of Jesus Christ of Latter-day Saints worked there.

Most days before or after work, I was out on the street meeting people and inviting them to come to our center to have dinner and hear an introductory lecture. We would often give street lectures, but what we had to offer was more than ideas. It was also a way of relating to each other. People were more likely to come to a workshop after experiencing the caring environment of our center than if we just extended the invitation on the street.

To meet people, we went out in pairs in public places like the University of California at Berkeley. Initially, it was difficult for me to start a conversation with strangers without feeling I was trying to impose something on them. I learned to listen to people, find their interests, and connect what was important to them to the work we were doing. This created a smooth transition to an invitation to learn more about our work.

Most of the people who accepted our invitations for dinner were young travelers. One afternoon on Telegraph Avenue, just off the Berkeley campus, my partner and I met a young man named Howard. He was from Ohio, where he worked for his parents in a hardware store. We talked for a while on the sidewalk, and then he walked back with us to the Hearst Street house.

Our evening programs started with dinner, followed by entertainment, an introductory lecture, and an invitation to attend our workshop. Frequently, I participated in the entertainment. I would stand in front of the small gathering and give a rousing rendition of an old favorite like "Without a Song."[2] Howard liked what he saw, accepted our invitation, and went to the workshop.

Following our weekend workshops, many of our guests stayed for a seven-day training. During those seven days, we set aside time for private prayer. Some of the guests had never offered a verbal prayer. At the meal following this prayer time, the new people had an opportunity to share. Everyone told a different story. One young man prayed and saw a deer when he looked up. For him, seeing the deer was a sign from God. Another young man prayed and found forgiveness for his father. He was one of seven children, and his father did not connect with him. Even though his father was in the home, this young man had felt abandoned. He said his prayer softened his heart, and he found compassion for his father. Hearing what it was like for our guests to pray for the first time warmed my heart. Howard stayed for the seven days and even felt the tug to stay longer; however, he returned to Ohio at the end of the week. I was sad to see him go.

To advance our purposes, we set "conditions." A condition had a specific period, a defined purpose, and an associated activity such as service, study, fasting, or prayer. Our conditions brought the power of God to an area of concern. I was continuously setting my own conditions and joining with others in setting conditions to move our work forward.

As a result of those conditions, I saw miracles. Sometimes it was something internal like a change of heart. Sometimes it was something external. On one occasion, I set a condition with my co-workers in the carpet cleaning company. Reverend Moon wanted to address world hunger by purchasing a fishing trawler. We set a goal to raise money to buy the trawler. One night, we prayed we would receive a request for carpet cleaning under an existing government contract. The next morning, I received a phone call at the office to schedule

$20,000 worth of carpet cleaning at an Air Force base. We gave God the glory for His response to our prayer. One of our local leaders said, "We don't believe in miracles, we depend on them." It was true. As we fulfilled our conditions and strived to achieve our goals, life was one miracle after another.

In the 1970s, the Unification Church and Reverend Moon were often in the media. Much of the coverage was negative. I was familiar with negative press from my days as a student at BYU when the media portrayed the Church of Jesus Christ of Latter-day Saints as racially prejudiced. To me, the negative news about the Unification Church was one more failure of the media to represent a religion fairly.

The media did not understand the hearts and minds of Reverend Moon or committed members of the Unification Church. They either discredited the Unification Church and Reverend Moon by using disaffected members as definitive authorities, or they presented Reverend Moon as a con man by distorting facts and spreading malicious rumors to support their claims.

Negativity was a fact of our lives as Unificationists. The press gave us the nickname "Moonies." It was a demeaning term that stuck. From time to time as I raised money selling flowers on a street corner, a passerby would shout, "Moonie!" I didn't take offense. They had no idea who I was or what I was doing.

One critique of the Unification Church was that its leaders forced the members to do things. This was not my experience! I accepted requests and followed commands conscious that my actions were consistent with my commitment to fulfilling God's purposes. I was never forced to do anything. For me, the intentionality of our activities resulted in individual empowerment and collective effectiveness. Without the support and encouragement of my brothers and sisters in faith, I would never have been part of a prosperous carpet cleaning company, and I would never have become successful in door-to-door sales.

One of the consequences of the negative media was that it fostered parental anxiety and the practice of deprogramming. Deprogramming cost thousands of dollars. It included abducting adult members of our church and attempting to break their faith. Deprogrammers contacted my parents, but they refused to have me deprogrammed. Even though they did not approve of my participation in the Unification Church, they allowed me the freedom to find my own way.

When deprogrammers abducted my friends, I didn't know if I would ever see them again. One day my friends were fully part of my life, and the next, they were gone. Some of my abducted friends renounced the Unification Church and spoke out against it. Others returned, and we welcomed them back. After the abduction of my friend John Abelseth, I offered many tearful prayers for his safety. When he returned, we hugged and wept for joy.

Whatever we did, as individuals or as a whole, whether it was fundraising, witnessing, or service of any kind, I saw it as fulfilling Reverend Moon's vision of uniting the world centered on God. Despite being imprisoned in North Korea as a young man and again in the United States in the 1980s, he kept his vision of a God-centered world fresh and alive by initiating innovative ways to unite people and to resolve historical conflicts.

I actively participated in the Oakland Family until August 1979 when I became a student at the Unification Theological Seminary. At the end of a day of carpet cleaning, I called from our office in East Oakland to the Hearst Street house to report on the day's work. In that phone call, I received an invitation to attend a twenty-one-day workshop in New York. I went back to Berkeley and met with the local church president, Dr. Mose Durst, to learn more about the workshop.

Dr. Durst told me the workshop was for prospective seminary students. This was a dream come true! Ever since I had first heard about the Unification Theological Seminary in 1976, I had wanted to receive seminary training. Eager to discover the life waiting for me as a seminarian, I went straight from my interview with Dr. Durst to the airport and took an overnight flight to New York. The next day, I joined the seminary workshop.

The Oakland Family grounded me in my new faith. There I learned to love sharing Reverend Moon's message. I found fulfillment in working in cooperation with others to build God's kingdom on earth, I learned to persevere in the face of hardships, and I thrilled in the many opportunities to sing. From my training in fundraising, I learned how to raise money anytime, anywhere. The Oakland Family empowered me, prepared me for future challenges, and gifted me with good friends and sweet memories.

Notes:

1. Moon, S. (1977). *Divine Principle.* New York: Holy Spirit Association for the Unification of World Christianity.

2. Rose, B., & Eliscu, E. (Lyricists). & Youmans, V. (Composer). (1929). "Without a Song." New York: Miller Music.

CHAPTER 12

TRAINING TO BE A UNIFICATION CHURCH LEADER

I ARRIVED AT the seminary at dusk and joined the workshop participants gathered in a circle outside. At first, I couldn't see everyone's faces. As my eyes adjusted to the darkness, I recognized one person after another I knew from the Oakland Family. The Oakland Family was the most productive center in the country in bringing members into the Unification Church. Hundreds of members joined the Oakland Family and from there went to serve in many capacities throughout the United States. About half of the seventy participants in the workshop were people I knew from their time with the Unification Church in California. Among them was the young woman who had greeted me on the street in Palo Alto in 1976. I took comfort in being among friends.

Although we were all followers of Reverend Moon, our assignments before the workshop were not necessarily with the Unification Church. There were participants from a campus ministry called the Collegiate Association for the Research of Principles (CARP); the National Mobile Fundraising Teams, which raised money to fund the outreach of the Unification Church in the United States; and other organizations sponsored by Reverend Moon. One of these other organizations was News World Communications, the publisher of the *New York City Tribune* and, later, *The Washington Times.*

Many of the attendees were already successful leaders. Leaving their positions to enroll in the seminary created a vacuum of leadership in their organizations. Their superiors had reluctantly sent them to the seminary. Our destiny was to be future leaders of the Unification Movement under the personal direction of Reverend Moon. None of the seminary graduates would be returning to their former positions of leadership.

The purpose of the twenty-one-day workshop was to ground us in the fundamentals of the Unification Church. In the spirit of going back to basics, we attended *Divine Principle* lectures. Additional lectures on "Victory over Communism" provided content new to me. The Unification Church was staunchly anti-communist. Reverend Moon had been confined to a forced labor camp in response to his ministry in Pyongyang, the capital of North Korea. He saw one person after another die from the adverse conditions in the camp. He knew the impact of the God-denying ideology of communism personally. The vision of a faith-based alternative to communism inspired me, and I knew I wanted to contribute to the cause of anti-communism. Upon completion of the workshop, we quickly transitioned into our first term as students.

Seminary culture was different than the Oakland Family, and I had difficulty adapting. I had come from a life driven by a strict schedule and communal devotional activities. Now I was expected to be independent in managing my time and self-generate my life of faith. In the transition, I missed the life I had left behind.

Before becoming a student at the Unification Theological Seminary, I knew very little about the faculty. I discovered that they were perhaps the most diverse and well-qualified scholars at any seminary in the world. Our Old Testament professor was a Jewish rabbi. We studied the writings of the early Christian fathers with a Greek Orthodox scholar. Our philosophy professor was a Catholic with a degree from the Sorbonne. A biblical scholar with the Reformed Church in America tutored us in the New Testament. We learned to preach from a Methodist minister with a PhD in Biblical studies. Reverend Moon intentionally assembled this unique faculty to give the future leaders of the Unification Church an inclusive perspective on religion, particularly Christianity. His vision was to prepare us to create bridges between religions as a foundation for the unification of the world centered on God. Reverend Moon did not intend the seminary to reinforce a conservative, narrowly defined agenda.

Our training in interfaith work included church visitations on Sundays. Vans from the seminary took us to churches all over the Hudson Valley. Each student went to a different church. I wanted to attend a congregation of Latter-day Saints. An upperclassman was already visiting the closest congregation, the Kingston Ward, so I started attending the Poughkeepsie Ward, thirty miles away.

The members of the ward welcomed me. After a couple of weeks, the Church Education Director invited me to have dinner with his family. He was responsible for gospel instruction for teenagers and young adults in a large geographic area. The following Sunday, a friend of mine came with me, and we went to the director's home for dinner. His family embraced us. In our conversations, they respected our religious views and communicated their beliefs with clarity and conviction. His children impressed us with their knowledge of the gospel. The warmth and goodwill they extended to us left me with a lasting memory of our time together.

In my first term at the seminary, I witnessed the abduction of one of my friends. I saw him get in the car with his parents and drive away. I found out later they had turned him over to deprogrammers. I was angry when I found out he was detained in an attempt to break his faith. I went to the chapel on campus and poured out my heart to God on his behalf. My tears flowed, and still, I kept praying. Then a calm came over me—he would be all right. In my mind's eye, I had an image of one of my father's big tanned hands. I knew that just as God had watched over me through my father in my youth, God was watching over my friend. A few days later, he returned, ready to continue his seminary training. Heavenly Father had answered my prayer.

A few weeks later, I was walking down the hallway near the entrance to the seminary building, and I saw two missionaries with the Church of Jesus Christ of Latter-day Saints approaching me. As I greeted them, I noticed the name tag of one of them read Elder Meservy. I told him I had taken an Old Testament class from Professor Keith Meservy at BYU. He said, "Professor Meservy is my father." We exchanged a few words, and they were on their way. It was a passing encounter that made a lasting impression on me.

Just before Thanksgiving, the seminary students served as staff members at the International Conference for the Unity of the Sciences in Century City, California. Reverend Moon sponsored this annual conference to build bridges between scientific disciplines, which were often isolated from each other. Hundreds of world-renowned scholars presented papers on a wide range of topics. Serving on the staff of the conference was part of our seminary training. Reverend Moon wanted us to learn to relate to people from all walks of life, including accomplished scholars. During the conference, I worked in guest services. As part of my duties, I met and spoke with several Nobel laureates. They impressed me with their dedication to making a difference in their fields of expertise.

After the conference, we returned to the East Coast and spent December fundraising to help pay for our seminary education. I was with a fundraising team that worked in the New York City area. We went from staying at the Century Plaza Hotel in Los Angeles, with all its amenities, to fundraising on the streets of New York City. We sold one-dollar bags of peanuts during the day and slept on the floor of church centers at night. My fundraising captain knew his way around New York City, and before long, we were able to triple our income by changing our product from peanuts to framed prints. I was proud of our contribution to funding the seminary.

On December 14, 1979, the day after her fifty-eighth birthday, my mother's battle with cancer ended. Since the beginning of 1976, when I joined the Unification Church, I had seen my family only two or three times. On those visits and through occasional phone calls, I followed the progress of my mother's cancer treatment. Even though she was near death the last time I spoke with her, news of her passing stunned me. I asked to return home for her funeral. The seminary leader in charge counseled me not to go. He thought it would be better for the formation of my faith to persevere in our fundraising campaign rather than to take the time to be with my family. I had seen other members visit their families and never return. I knew this was part of his concern.

On the outside, I accepted his counsel and continued fundraising. On the inside, I was grieving, and my fundraising was halfhearted. Nevertheless, staying on task allowed me to process my loss. The consolation I received from other seminary students also helped me deal with my grief. A couple of weeks after her death, I was waiting in front of a Dunkin' Donuts in Port Chester, New York for the van to pick me up at the end of a day of fundraising. As I stood in the light of a street lamp, I was able to feel the pain over the loss of my mother and allow my tears to flow.

Back at the seminary for the winter quarter, I had the idea that the Unification Church could benefit from the teaching methods of the Church of Jesus Christ of Latter-day Saints. With this in mind, I called the bishop of the Kingston Ward and asked him if he would send someone to the seminary who could show us how to teach the way Latter-day Saints taught. He accepted my request and sent Carl Markle.

Carl was a brilliant man, well versed in the beliefs of a wide range of Christian churches. He learned what other people believed to better share the gospel. On his first visit, we explored what he could do to help us teach effectively. He decided he would read the *Divine Principle* and then teach from it using the instructional methods of the Church of Jesus Christ of Latter-day Saints.

When he returned, he powerfully taught key concepts of the *Divine Principle*. Impressed with his presentation, the dean of students asked Carl if he would teach a course the next term entitled "Preparing Teaching Materials." Carl accepted her offer and taught under her supervision. It was a great course in which I learned how to simplify concepts, choose relevant visual images, and lead an engaging discussion.

Once when Carl was at the seminary, I told him I wasn't feeling well. Carl responded by asking me if I would like a priesthood blessing. The Church of Jesus Christ of Latter-day Saints authorizes righteous priesthood holders to give blessings of healing. I was familiar with priesthood blessings from BYU, though I had never had one. Confident in his capacity as a priesthood holder, I asked Carl to give me a blessing. As I sat in a chair, he placed his hands on my head and pronounced a blessing on me. I will never forget the effect. For the following three days, my heart was free. There was a bounce in my step, and I was genuinely joyful. That experience created an enduring memory of the power of a priesthood blessing.

Carl had a beautiful tenor voice, and he knew I liked to sing. He proposed we sing a duet at one of our daily morning worship services. I welcomed his suggestion, and we chose to sing "Be Thou My Vision." In front of the student body, Carl sang harmony as we joined in song. The words of the second verse remained in my heart afterward: "Be Thou my Wisdom, and Thou my true Word, I ever with Thee and Thou with me, Lord, Thou my great Father, I Thy true son, Thou in me dwelling, and I with Thee one."[1]

I attended church with Carl at the Kingston Ward from time to time, and I got to know his family. At Easter, his wife Grace gave me a gift. It was just a basket of candies, but it communicated powerfully: "You are loved."

In May 1980, just before the summer break, Carl violated my trust. He knew I planned on having Reverend Moon match me to a member of the Unification Church. In spite of knowing my intention, he asked me to go on a double date with him and his wife. He was going to set me up with a member of the Kingston Ward as my date. I was outraged. I told him he was out of line. He responded by saying, "I only want you to have the freedom to choose your own wife."

I told him, "I don't need you to create choices for me." In the few months we had known each other, I had come to respect and trust him. It seemed like he was using my trust to manipulate me.

About that time, David Kim, the seminary president, told me my interest in the Church of Jesus Christ of Latter-day Saints was interfering with my preparations to be a Unification Church leader. In spite of Reverend Moon's guidance to follow your leader, I resisted President Kim's advice. After some reflection, I took President Kim's counsel to Heavenly Father in prayer. My heart softened, I humbled myself, and I chose to take his coaching. I stopped seeing Carl, and I stopped meeting with Latter-day Saints.

During the summer of 1980, the seminary students participated in an outreach organized by CARP, the Collegiate Association for the Research of Principles, to find young people interested in our work. We went out on the streets of New York City and invited people we met to the national headquarters of the Unification Church located on 43rd Street just off Fifth Avenue. Some of our guests found our ideas appealing and signed up for our workshop at a camp in Massachusetts.

Before long, I was leading the workshop graduates in Boston, where there was a CARP center large enough to accommodate them. Leading them was rewarding. I taught them how to fundraise, drove the fundraising van, ordered and picked up flowers to sell, counseled them individually, taught them how to street witness, and contributed to the entertainment at our evening programs. I was able to handle it when there were five participants, but by the end of the summer, I was working with forty trainees. I didn't ask for the help I needed, and I didn't pace myself. I returned to the seminary in September exhausted. I began the school year without enthusiasm.

One of my friends, Thomas Ward, noticed my lackluster attitude and asked me what was going on. I told him that when it came time to pray, I couldn't find anything to say. He suggested I write my prayers. It had not occurred to me that writing down my prayers would provide the connection to God I needed. I set a condition to put down on paper what I otherwise would have verbalized for forty minutes a day for twenty-one days. Through the daily writing of my prayers, I expressed the unspoken desires of my heart and regained my spark and enthusiasm.

That year, there was an International Conference for the Unity of the Sciences in Miami. After staffing the conference, all the seminarians went fundraising for the rest of the winter break. I was on a team working in Detroit, Michigan. Near the end of December, we returned to New York, along with all the other fundraising teams, to participate in the upcoming matching.

The matching was an opportunity for Reverend Moon to personally select a spouse for us from among other church members. Like most seminary students, I wasn't yet matched. In 1979 there had been another matching, and some of my friends accepted matches at that time. I could see my future as I saw them with their fiancées. Helen was the fiancée of my friend John Abelseth. I saw harmony and peace in their relationship. Encouraged by their example, I was ready to find out who Reverend Moon would select for me.

He prepared us for the matching by teaching us one of the principles of the ancient tradition of matching. When young couples trust their parents to find them a match, they start the marriage with a stronger bond to their parents than to their spouse. In times of marital challenge, the wife turns to her parents, and the husband turns to his parents to gain the vision and commitment to work things out. In our case, our mutual love and respect for Reverend Moon and his wife, as our spiritual parents, would serve as a stabilizing influence in our marriages. With this principle in mind, I looked forward to the matching.

All the matching candidates gathered in the Unification Church-owned New Yorker Hotel. Everyone had spent at least three years in full-time service with the Unification Church or one of its affiliated organizations. The candidates were men and women of faith and proven commitment. We crowded into the Grand Ballroom and sat on the floor. After a prayer and hymn singing, the matching began. Reverend Moon had us move back and create an aisle down the middle of the ballroom so he could walk among us.

President Kim had his own ideas about matches for the seminary students and at one point advised Reverend Moon. His attempted intervention riled Reverend Moon, and he told President Kim to mind his own business. Right after that exchange, Reverend Moon asked Amy, a seminary student, to stand. He then looked around the room and chose me as her match. That day, Reverend Moon matched 853 couples one at a time.

Amy and I had first met at a weekend workshop in California in 1977. She was now a first-year seminary student, and we had participated in a few activities together. At no time had it ever crossed my mind we might have a future together as husband and wife.

Part of our commitment in accepting our match was to maintain our chastity and focus on our respective mission responsibilities rather than on each other. We dutifully kept our distance. We only occasionally talked with each other or did things together. One time, we put on a picnic for people in Newburgh whom we had met doing door-to-door service. As we were getting ready to go, I made sure we had all the food we needed, and Amy confirmed we had all the necessary sports equipment. Amy was a natural athlete and loved all kinds of sports. As I thought about the differences between us, I wondered why Reverend Moon had put us together. I didn't question his wisdom; instead, I was looking for insight into who we were as a couple. I concluded our differences complemented and completed each other.

In the spring of 1981, I saw two professors I knew from Brigham Young University on campus. What a surprise! They had come to the seminary to attend an interfaith conference. We warmly greeted each other. They had no idea I was with the Unification Church. John Staley and I had become friends because his office in the Department of Social Work at BYU was near my office as a graduate research assistant. He had a notable conversion story. Before he met his wife and joined the Church of Jesus Christ of Latter-day Saints in the late 1960s, he had been a Catholic priest. The other professor, John Seggar, had been my professor for several courses, my supervisor as a research assistant, and my adviser for my master's thesis.

Some of the scholars who attended our interfaith conferences kept the Unification Church at arm's length and behaved like observers. Not John Staley and John Seggar. They were willing to participate in our worship services and discover something for themselves. Dr. Staley got up early on Sunday morning to attend our 5:00 a.m. prayer meeting, and Dr. Seggar said our view of prayer as a means of moving the heart of God inspired him to explore a new dimension of prayer in his own life. It moved me that they were open to finding value in our faith tradition.

The conference they attended included small group meetings. Scholars from various religious backgrounds had an opportunity to dialog with Unification Church scholars and seminary students. The event ended at noon on Sunday, and Drs. Seggar and Staley had arranged to stay another day. They planned on visiting Camphill Village, a self-sustaining community for adults with developmental disabilities. Dr. Staley wanted to explore the Camphill model to get ideas for creating a home for his stepson, who needed the support of a similar living environment. I arranged for a car, and the three of us spent Monday learning about this empowering community. When he returned to Utah, members of the Unification Church helped Dr. Staley set up a home for adults with developmental disabilities in Utah. This interfaith mutuality inspired me.

In addition to interfaith dialogs like the one these BYU professors attended, there had been several meetings with scholars with a particular religious viewpoint, such as the Evangelical-Unification Dialog and the Orthodox-Unification Dialog. I started thinking about organizing a conference at the seminary that would be a Mormon-Unification Dialog.

There were times when Reverend Moon came to meet with us as seminary students. On one of his visits, we gathered to meet with him in the open air beside the pond. He leaned against the split rail fence surrounding the pond as we sat on the ground in front of him. He began by asking for someone to sing, and I volunteered. I sang, "The Exodus Song."[2] When I finished, Reverend Moon coached me to sing with the power of rushing water. Later, I learned he counseled a wide range of world leaders and many church members on how to make the most of their abilities.

I graduated from the seminary in June 1981. Studying with religious educators from various religious traditions, meeting Nobel laureates, and bonding with other seminarians with diverse backgrounds in church service gave me a new vision for what I wanted to accomplish. I no longer saw inviting people to follow Reverend Moon as my only objective. My plans now included participating in the creation of a network of religious and humanitarian projects that would unite people around a vision of one world under God. With this perspective, I was eager to leave the seminary and get to work.

Following graduation, I attended a 120-day workshop with my classmates and Unification Church leaders from around the world. This workshop grounded future and existing church leaders in our fundamental teachings and outreach activities. The workshop consisted of forty days of lectures, forty days of street witnessing, and forty days of fundraising. The best part of the forty days of lectures was listening to Japanese and Korean leaders who had been with Reverend Moon for many years. They shared inspiring accounts of perseverance and faith.

From among the many speakers, Won Pil Kim stood out. He had been at Reverend Moon's side since the 1940s and knew his heart. One morning, I went into a small prayer room, and kneeling there alone was Reverend Won Pil Kim. I knelt down with him and offered my own prayer as his whispered expressions of his heart gave me a hint of his deep love for God. The workshop served as a powerful culmination of my training to become a Unification Church leader.

Notes:

1. Forgail, D. (8th c.). "Be Thou My Vision." In *The New English Hymnal.* Norwich, England: Canterbury Press, 1998.

2. Boone, P. (Lyricist). & Gold, E. (Composer). (1952). "The Exodus Song." New York: Chappell

CHAPTER 13

A MOONIE AMONG THE MORMONS

ON COMPLETING THE 120-day workshop, I accepted an assignment as the CARP leader at the University of Illinois Circle Campus in Chicago. It was just what I was looking for in a leadership opportunity. I led a small group of members in meeting students and promoting our campus activities. When the university dismissed for the Christmas break, we all went on the road fundraising.

In January 1982, I accepted a reassignment from CARP to the national headquarters in Manhattan as an assistant to the public affairs director. I learned how to write press releases and monitor media references to the Unification Church or Reverend Moon. If any news agency published a negative or inaccurate article, we responded with a letter. Many of the headquarters staff were dear friends I knew from the Oakland Family, and it was great to be working with them again.

An essential part of our outreach involved establishing Home Churches. A Home Church was an area of 360 homes. The intention was to get to know the people in those homes and find ways to serve them. Through service, the person who created the Home Church would demonstrate the love of God. Reverend Moon declared the kingdom of heaven would be established through the proliferation of Home Churches.

The leader of the Home Church activities in New York City was Reverend Won Pil Kim. I volunteered to be the national headquarters representative to his weekly Home Church meetings. It was a privilege to work with him. He had an inspiring enthusiasm for Home Church work and a deep love for people. But as much as I enjoyed the activities at headquarters, I wanted to get out in the field.

There was an opening for a state leader in Utah, and I asked Dr. Durst, who was then the national president, if I could assume that responsibility. A state leader was responsible for representing the Unification Church and creating relationships with people in their assigned state. While I had been a student at BYU, I benefited greatly from the generosity of Latter-day Saints as they shared the value of their lives of faith with me. I wanted to return to Utah and reciprocate by sharing with them the value of the Unification Church.

At the beginning of February, Dr. Durst authorized me to be the state leader of Utah. Eager to share my joy, I called Amy at the seminary. She encouraged me to move ahead with my new assignment. I had no training specific to being a state leader, yet I was ready to discover the challenges and blessings waiting for me.

When I accepted the position, I had no money to get to Utah. Over the next two days, I put my training to work, and I went door-to-door fundraising with boxes of peanut brittle and caramel clusters. There was always candy on hand to sell, and all I had to do was pay for it after I sold it. Three days later, I had made enough money for a plane ticket to Colorado, and I was on my way to Denver. Denver was the regional center of the Unification Church for several states including Utah.

I joined a fundraising team of Denver center members and spent a couple of weeks in the mountains of Colorado selling Jolly Rancher candy in decorative glass jars. I was grateful I could work with the team as I raised money to start my ministry in Utah. The camaraderie and the regimen of the team made fundraising an exciting adventure.

When I arrived in Utah, I initially stayed with old friends from the Self-Realization Fellowship. We had started our meditation group more than ten years earlier, and we had not seen each other since I left for California in 1973. We had a great time catching up, and they told me that our group continued to meditate together weekly. What a joy to discover our group was still viable! Within days of my arrival, I found an apartment in Salt Lake City. I thanked my friends for their hospitality and moved into my new apartment.

It had been at least a year since the previous state leader had left and put all the audio-visual equipment and literature from the former Unification Church center in storage. I retrieved the materials and set up my apartment as a church center. At the time, I was the only member of the Unification Church in the state. I knew a member whose parents lived in Ogden, Utah, but the member herself was serving in New York. At one point, a national fundraising team with the Unification Church passed through Salt Lake City, and there was a college student who was with CARP, but for the purpose of my work, I was entirely on my own.

One of the first things I did was contact a friend of the Unification Church who was formerly a Latter-day Saint. I first met him when he came to visit the Unification Theological Seminary in 1979. When I arrived in Utah, I visited him and explained I wanted to establish a Home Church where leaders of the Church of Jesus Christ of Latter-day Saints lived. He gave me a general idea of the location of their homes.

With this information, I went to the Church's Visitors Center at Temple Square to pray. In that sacred place, I prayed that I would choose a Home Church area that would allow my efforts to have the greatest impact on Latter-day Saints. From Temple Square, I went to the neighborhood my friend described and mapped out 360 homes.

To prepare for my door-to-door work, I had a badge made with "Unification Church" printed underneath my name. I put it on, and I went about my work. Wearing a badge with my name and affiliation was not the custom for Unificationists. I was imitating Latter-day Saints serving as missionaries who wore name tags. Like them, I proudly displayed my name and the church I represented.

As I knocked on doors, I quickly discovered the people I met assumed my sole purpose was to try to convert them. Yes, it would have been a thrill to find someone interested in the Unification Church, but that was a secondary purpose. My primary objective was to build relationships based on common interests, which could develop into a contribution to the community.

In my initial visit to my Home Church area, I had two adventures. After knocking on a few doors, a man invited me into his home to meet his family. He introduced himself as the local bishop. He was the bishop of the ward that included the homes in my chosen area. He and his family were welcoming and respectful.

After visiting with the bishop and his family, I continued going door to door. About an hour later, two police cars pulled up with their lights flashing. I presented my ID, and they detained me briefly. Soon the officers withdrew, and I went about my business of knocking on doors.

On Sunday, I attended the ward meetings. More than three hundred people packed the chapel, and I found a seat in the back. After the opening hymn and prayer, the bishop got up and said he was aware a man had been knocking on doors and creating a nuisance in the neighborhood. No one seemed to notice I was the one he was talking about. He added, "He is not a threat."

After the main meeting, I attended a Sunday School class taught by Congressman Dan Marriott. Brother[1] Marriott accepted me for who I was and welcomed me. In the third hour of meetings, I met with the Elders Quorum. Most of these men were about my age, with families and demanding jobs. They didn't know what to think when I introduced myself as the state leader of the Unification Church in Utah.

I had thought people would notice I was not a member of the congregation and introduce themselves. For the most part, everyone was busy with their families, friends, and church duties. On my first Sunday, I didn't see anyone other than the bishop whom I had met in my door-to-door work, and

I didn't have any extended conversations. Nevertheless, I was confident I could find someone interested in an activity sponsored by the Unification Church or with whom I could create a project of our own.

I continued to attend ward meetings on Sundays and to reach out to the people living in my Home Church area during the week. Often in the morning, I went on a prayer walk. As I walked through the neighborhood, I prayed in my heart for the people who lived there. To be of service, I picked up litter. Even though there wasn't much litter, it was my way of doing something for the people whom I had chosen to love.

While I was on a morning prayer walk, I noticed a car pull up to one of the homes, and President Marion G. Romney, a counselor to the president of the Church, came out and got in the car. I presumed he was on his way to the Church Office Building, where he would attend to the business of the Church. In answer to my prayers, I had chosen homes where the leaders of the Church of Jesus Christ of Latter-day Saints lived. Not only did President Romney live in my Home Church area, but Spencer W. Kimball, the president of the Church, had his home there. He was in poor health and for practical purposes lived in the Hotel Utah.

I had a breakthrough in my door-to-door work on Thursday evening before Easter. As it was getting dark and beginning to snow, I knocked on the kitchen door of a home on Princeton Avenue. The family invited me in to join them in coloring Easter eggs. As we dyed eggs, I got to know John and Florence Stamm and their young daughter. John was a successful missionary. Over the years, he contributed to bringing many people into the Church. Florence was an excellent vocalist and had been a member of the Tabernacle Choir. When I told her I had voice training, she invited me to join the ward choir, and I accepted. I thought it would be a good way to serve the people in my area.

Soon I was singing in the choir. A few weeks after I had sat in the back listening to the bishop explaining I was not a threat, I was in front of the congregation behind President

Romney and the ward leadership singing. However, a few weeks later, a counselor in the bishopric pulled me aside to tell me I could no longer be in the choir. The bishop's counselor explained that several members of the ward had complained about my participation in the choir. The bishop was out of town, and the burden fell upon him to address their concern. He confided in me that it wasn't easy for him to remove me from the choir. He said he felt it was in the best interest of maintaining harmony in the ward if I didn't sing in the choir. As gracious as he was in his delivery, it wasn't easy to receive what he said. I wanted to sing in the choir.

Reverend Moon taught that rejection is a blessing because it identifies who you need to love. I learned the man who asked me to leave the choir and his wife had just adopted a baby boy. With Reverend Moon's counsel in mind, I sent them some clothes for their son with a note of congratulations. I prayed they would receive the gift as an expression of goodwill.

I went to Utah to return the love members of the Church of Jesus Christ of Latter-day Saints had poured out upon me while I was at BYU. I was harmless and well-intentioned. If more members of the ward had known my heart, I am confident they would have seen me as an asset, and they would have been happy to have me stay in the choir.

My presence drew the attention of several former mission presidents, and they invited me to meet with them. These were men of faith and accomplishment. In an atmosphere of mutual respect, they shared with me the gospel and their testimonies, and I shared with them my beliefs and my purpose for being in Utah. I appreciated their personal attention, but our meeting had no lasting impact on them or me.

One of my adventures in Utah was speaking to the graduate students in a comparative religion class at Brigham Young University. I had known the professor, Spencer J. Palmer, when I was a student at BYU. When I renewed our acquaintance, he asked me to speak to his class on the topic

"The Unique Contributions of the Unification Church." It was a pleasure to do so. Citing and expounding on the commentaries of scholars regarding the Unification Church, I provided an informed overview of its contributions. At the time, Reverend Moon was organizing a student tour to the religious capitals of the world. This was an all-expense-paid trip in which participants visited many countries including Egypt, Israel, India, Korea, and Japan. I described the excursion in my lecture, and two of the students expressed interest, submitted their applications, and went on the tour.

My friendship with John Stamm grew, and I asked him what he thought I could do to serve the neighborhood. At the intersection of Herbert and Princeton Avenues, there was an unattractive wasted space. He thought the area was big enough to create a circular traffic island, which could be planted with flowers. I wrote to the city and asked them to explore the possibility of a traffic island there. The highway department came out to measure the dimensions of the intersection and wrote back that the intersection was not big enough to put in an island. I dropped the matter, thinking I had done all I could do. More than twenty years later on a visit to Salt Lake City, I drove through the neighborhood and saw that a traffic island had been installed just as John had envisioned.

John and I became frequent companions. We weeded a field of vegetables at a Church-owned farm that raised food for those in need, and we provided service for a widow by preparing the soil in her garden for planting. In our conversations, John told me his wife Florence had the assignment to visit President Kimball's wife, Camilla. All the women in the Church had assignments to visit other women in their congregations. Knowing Florence, it was no surprise to me one of the women she visited was Sister Kimball. From my point of view, John and Florence were the embodiment of the love of God.

John and I also went to visit Dr. Cleon Skousen, a prominent member of the Church. We met with him at the offices of the National Center for Constitutional Studies, a politically conservative organization he founded. I had known of Dr. Skousen when I was a student at BYU, but I had never met him. He welcomed us, and he told us about his work. He mentioned he had friends in the Unification Church in New York with whom he planned to co-sponsor events to advance the work of his organization.

Dr. Skousen eventually contributed, in cooperation with Unification Church members, to several conferences designed to educate political and religious leaders about the flaws of communism and to offer a faith-based alternative. Dr. Skousen's involvement in those conferences validated my vision of people of faith working together in service of a shared concern. When what we have in common is the focus of our attention, our differences are not a barrier to relationships.

It was my responsibility as a state leader to create a visible presence of the Unification Church in Utah. In the time I worked there—from March until June 1982—I made my presence known at BYU and in the congregation of Latter-day Saints in my Home Church area. I met with Cleon Skousen and introduced myself to both Governor Scott Matheson and the mayor of Salt Lake City, Ted Wilson.

In June, I returned to New York City to assist with the preparations for the upcoming Unification Church wedding in Madison Square Garden on July 1, 1982. This would be my wedding to Amy and the wedding of 2,074 other couples! Members came from all over the world. Some had been matched from a picture and had never met their future spouses. Some even had to communicate with their matches through an interpreter because they did not speak the same language.

This mass wedding, or "Blessing," was intended to create bonds, not just between individual couples, but to unite us in a brotherhood of families dedicated to establishing the kingdom of heaven on earth. We considered the breakdown of the family to be central to all social problems. By uniting with other couples and publicly advocating for families centered on

God, we declared our commitment to family as the cornerstone of a divinely empowered society.

Amy and I were in touch through letters and phone calls, yet we had not seen each other in six months. When we reunited, we were dressed for the occasion. Staged in wedding attire, all 4,150 brides and grooms were ready when the event began. The brides wore white wedding dresses and stood to the left of their grooms in their dark-blue suits. With amazing precision, the Blessing proceeded as planned. Throughout the ceremony, there was a deep feeling of God's loving presence.

Amy and I had very few guests. Amy's mother came from Jamestown, New York, and my twenty-one-year-old brother Bert came from California. Bert and I were close. This was not the first time he had come to visit me. Bert had made the trip when I was at the seminary as well. This time, he came not only to attend the wedding but also because he loved New York City. Carl and one of his friends from the Kingston Ward were our only other guests.

After the ceremony, all the couples and their guests gathered back in Madison Square Garden for spectacular entertainment. The Blessing activities passed quickly, and within days, Amy left on the tour of the religious capitals of the world. She was on the staff of the trip that included the two BYU students I had invited.

Ours was not a traditional marriage in which the bride and groom go off on a honeymoon afterward. Most of the couples, including Amy and I, were in a separation period in preparation to starting our family life. Amy and I did not expect to begin our life as husband and wife for several years. We didn't even see each other again for months.

After the Blessing, I went to the regional headquarters in Denver. The regional director felt there was greater strength in numbers, and I accepted his request to stay in Denver. I joined the members of the Denver center in street witnessing, staffing workshops for prospective members, and fundraising. It was a disappointment to find that Home Church work was not a focus of the outreach in Denver. I missed meeting people in their homes and serving them as I had in Utah. On the other hand, I enjoyed the companionship of the Denver center members after working alone in Utah.

Notes:

1. Members of the Church refer to each other as Brother or Sister followed by their last name.

CHAPTER 14

A MORMON-UNIFICATION DIALOG

AT THE BEGINNING of 1983, six months after the Madison Square Garden Blessing, Reverend Moon reorganized the leadership of the Unification Church in the United States. He assigned seasoned Korean church leaders to each region. As national president, Dr. Durst had envisioned implementing the model he used in attracting members to the Oakland Family to expand membership throughout the country. This change to Korean leadership took our activities in another direction and required the state leaders to adapt to a different leadership style. When our newly designated regional leader arrived in Denver, he told me to plan a trip to Utah and arrange a meeting with a representative of the Church of Jesus Christ of Latter-day Saints.

We flew to Salt Lake City and met with the public affairs director of the Church. John Stamm set up the meeting for us, and the Church provided a Korean interpreter. The Korean leader and I met with John and Florence Stamm, the interpreter, and the public affairs director.

After we had all introduced ourselves, the Church representative expressed interest in the work of the Unification Church and the Korean leader responded. I then challenged the public affairs director by asking him if the welfare program of the Church predominately served the members of the Church. He acknowledged it did. I told him that neglecting the poor in the general population was inconsistent with the scriptures and represented a weakness in their program. Before he had a chance to comment, a notification of the death of Elder LeGrand Richards interrupted our meeting. Elder Richards had been one of the members of the Quorum of the Twelve Apostles, a principal leadership body of the Church. The public affairs director ended our meeting to prepare the press release. The timing of the announcement Elder Richard's death seemed divinely timed to get my attention.

In February, I traveled to New York for a meeting of Unification Church leaders. When Reverend Moon addressed us, he announced he was reassigning all of the state leaders. I reasoned he was doing this to shake up existing relationships so that we would be more receptive to the guidance of the new Korean leaders. I had made a request of Dr. Bo Hi Pak to join him in organizing conferences which provided an alternative to communism. During the preparations to reassign the state leaders, Dr. Pak asked Reverend Moon if I could work with him. Reverend Moon rejected the request. I dealt with my disappointment, and I accepted Reverend Moon's decision without protest.

One of the leaders wrote the names of all the states on small pieces of paper and put them in a bag. The state leaders lined up, and one by one drew out a slip of paper that disclosed their new state assignment. The one I picked read, "New York." What a change! I went from having no one under my direction as the state leader of Utah to overseeing more than one hundred full-time members.

Being the state leader of New York was a complicated responsibility. The leaders of the witnessing teams, fundraising teams, and the workshop in Massachusetts reported to me, as well as the local center leaders in Brooklyn, Queens, the Bronx, and Albany. I had new responsibilities for pastoral counseling, delivering Sunday sermons, and serving as a liaison between the Unification Church and organizations Reverend Moon sponsored in New York City. There was no manual to follow, and my training was entirely on the job. In addition to my many responsibilities, I participated in a prayer service at midnight and at 5:00 a.m. seven days a week.

I carried on, committed to rising to the challenge. I loved the work, even though I was tired most of the time.

In my position as the state leader, I had the opportunity to meet with Reverend Won Pil Kim for periodic Home Church meetings. In Home Church work we looked for the most difficult person to love and devoted ourselves to serving them. When they rejected us, we continued to serve them and patiently accept their complaints. We intended to win their hearts so that they would be receptive to our message. Reverend Kim had spent a lifetime following this pattern of loving difficult people, and he had an invigorating presence.

A story from his life that I keep in my heart relates to his dedication to church work. As part of the religious persecution of the Korean Unification Church in the 1950s, police came to his home to arrest him at 10:00 p.m., only to find he was not there. They returned to apprehend him at 3:00 a.m. They discovered he had come home, slept a couple of hours, and left again at 2:00 a.m. I heard many stories about Reverend Kim's extraordinary commitment. To me, he was a living miracle.

During my time as the state leader of New York, a missionary serving with the Church of Jesus Christ of Latter-day Saints took an interest in the Unification Church. This young man had been assigned to work in Westchester County and had met some members of the Unification Church. Impressed with them, he showed an interest in our beliefs and started to question his own faith. His interest in the Unification Church distracted him from his purpose and his mission leader, President Albert Choules, sent him home to his family.

The members who had met with this missionary told me what had happened, and I arranged to meet President Choules to foster goodwill. We met in his apartment near the Lincoln Center on Manhattan's Upper West Side. In the course of our conversation, I mentioned I had been in the Church Office Building in Salt Lake City in January, the day Elder LeGrand Richards died. When I said this, President Choules presented me with a book written by Elder Richards entitled *A Marvelous Work and a Wonder*.[1] Published in 1950, it had sold millions of copies. It was written to help people interested in the Church of Jesus Christ of Latter-day Saints understand the gospel. Elder Richards had signed the copy President Choules gave me. This book became a keepsake and a reminder of my personal connection to Elder Richards and my visit with President Choules.

A few weeks later, I was at the Unification Theological Seminary for a conference I had helped organize, the Mormon-Unification Dialog. During my 120-day training, I met with the educational director, Reverend Ken Sudo. In our interview, Reverend Sudo asked me, "How do you want to contribute to the Unification Movement as a leader?"

I told him, "I want to organize a Mormon-Unification Dialog." I explained to Reverend Sudo that I was not just interested in an academic conference. I wanted to open the way for Latter-day Saints to see the value of Reverend Moon's perspective. The meeting would not be an indirect approach to convert people or a means to promote Reverend Moon as a messianic figure. Reverend Sudo was supportive, and I took his endorsement as a call to action.

In the spring of 1982, while I was the state leader of Utah, I began preparing for the dialog. I made several visits to BYU to connect with faculty members I intended to invite. One of the people I met with was Jae R. Baillif, who was the academic vice president. Dr. Baillif was my professor for an introductory physics course in the spring of 1970. I remembered him well. Even though the class I took from him had been a large lecture class, he had called me into his office to ask my opinion about the course materials. That short interview stood out in my memory because he was the only professor who ever asked my opinion about his approach to teaching. He remembered me too, even before I reminded him of our conversation more than ten years earlier. When I told him I was with the Unification Church, he mentioned he had participated in one of the International Conferences for the Unity of the Sciences.

My next step to prepare for the Mormon-Unification Dialog was to send out letters of invitation to BYU professors. After receiving my invitation, one of the professors contacted Dr. Baillif to see if he thought faculty members might run the risk of compromising their integrity by accepting an invitation to an all-expense-paid conference. In the past, many professors from BYU, like Dr. Baillif, had attended various conferences sponsored by organizations inspired by Reverend Moon that were all-expense-paid events, such as the International Conference for the Unity of the Sciences and theological dialogs at the Unification Theological Seminary. This faculty member's question made it to the board of directors of Brigham Young University. The board of directors included the president of the Church, as well as members of the Quorum of the Twelve Apostles.

In response to the question, the board of directors clarified an existing policy by sending a memo to BYU faculty members. In the memo, the board reminded them they were not authorized to accept free travel and accommodations to attend conferences. It went on to say that BYU faculty members could only participate in such conferences if they paid their own way. All the BYU professors who had already accepted my invitation chose not to attend. It was a setback in my planning, yet I saw it as a success. My efforts had come to the attention of the highest leadership of the Church.

With renewed resolve, I started the invitational process over again. This time, I had the help of the sponsoring organization, the New Ecumenical Research Association (New ERA). Reverend Moon founded New ERA to create dialog and foster understanding between Unificationists and members of Christian churches. We started looking for Latter-day Saints who were scholars but who were not faculty members at a school funded by their church.

Once I became the state leader of New York, I wasn't able to devote much time to organizing the dialog. Thankfully, the New ERA staff and seminary students did the bulk of the work to prepare for the event. Through our combined efforts, a diverse group of eight scholars who were members of the Church of Jesus Christ of Latter-day Saints participated in the conference. They did not officially represent their church; they represented themselves. The participants included Dr. Richard Bushman, a professor of history at Columbia University, and his wife, Dr. Claudia Bushman, an American studies scholar; Dr. Gerald Jones, the Director of the Institute of Religion for the Church of Jesus Christ of Latter-day Saints at Yale University; and Peggy Fletcher, the editor of *Sunstone*, an independent magazine for Mormon studies.

The dialog began with a dinner on Friday night, April 22, 1983, and continued until midday on Sunday. Since the conference took place at the seminary where Amy was in her last year as a divinity student, I had a chance to see her, but we had very little time together during the conference weekend.

The Latter-day Saints who came wanted to learn about the methods the Unification Church used to attract new members. In the mid-1970s, thousands of young single adults in the United States made a full-time commitment to the Unification Church. Their interest in our witnessing methods resulted in a spirited conversation. It was a joy to engage with these distinguished educators on the topic of missionary work.

The Mormon-Unification Dialog was a culminating event for me in my interfaith work with the Church of Jesus Christ of Latter-day Saints. My duties as a church leader were all-consuming, and I didn't follow up with the participants to build on the experience we had together. What could have been the beginning of further dialog turned out to be only a passing encounter.

While I was the state leader of New York, I was frequently with Reverend Moon. I attended Reverend Moon's Sunday sermons, his speeches on church holidays, and periodic state leader meetings under his direction. Additionally, I attended smaller gatherings at his home in Irvington to celebrate birthdays in the Moon family. It was an honor to be with him.

He gave his speeches in Korean, and his interpreter was always a close associate whose first language was Korean. As Reverend Moon spoke, his interpreter stayed at his side as he moved back and forth in front of the gathering. During his speeches, he often made bold strokes with chalk on a large green blackboard to create graphics to illustrate his point. He was enthusiastic, animated, and spontaneous—sometimes calling for a response from the audience. During his talks, Reverend Moon would sometimes lean forward, put his hands on his knees, and look out with an engaging smile into the audience sitting on the floor in front of him.

His talks usually lasted four or five hours. Even though I was uncomfortable sitting on the floor for long periods, it was a small price to pay to have the privilege of being with him. My sense of connection to Reverend Moon was an extension of my relationship with my father. They were both born in February 1920. To me, they had similar personalities.

Toward the end of May 1983, while I was doing my laundry, I noticed a book on the folding table entitled *Burnout*. As I skimmed through the book, the symptoms of burnout struck home. Most significant to me were detachment and exhaustion. Even though I was surrounded by people, I had only a superficial connection to them. My constant fatigue had taken its toll, and I had very little energy. The book made several recommendations on how to mitigate the effects of burnout. If I followed the guidance the book offered, I would have to slow down, listen to my body, and give myself time to process the stressors in my life. The regional leader noticed I was worn out and told me to take it easy. I ignored his advice and the suggestions in the book. In spite of my detachment and exhaustion, I soldiered on.

Notes:

1. Richards, L. (1980). *A Marvelous Work and a Wonder.* Salt Lake City, Utah: Deseret Book.

CHAPTER 15

DEALING WITH BURNOUT

I CONTINUED AS the state leader of New York until July 1983. I then accepted an assignment as the leader of a traveling witnessing team. I led ten members in a series of three-week campaigns. Reverend Moon sent similar teams all across the country.

We began with twenty-one days in New York City. We then moved on to Newark, New Jersey, followed by Columbus, Ohio; Philadelphia, Pennsylvania; Dover, Delaware; and New Haven, Connecticut. We had a demanding regimen of street witnessing, public service projects, meetings with public officials, and fundraising with flowers. In Newark, I wore myself out, and I had to rest for a couple of days.

In Philadelphia, our Korean leader was Mrs. Hyo Won Eu. She had joined the Unification Church as a college student in the 1950s. She was the widow of the man who had worked closely with Reverend Moon to write the *Divine Principle*. She was candid and accessible. She knew who she was, and I knew she cared about us. Working with her was wonderful!

Spiritually renewed, I was ready to give my best in the next city on our tour. Our twenty-one-day campaign in Dover began on November 3, 1983. The state leader and I created a plan, which included the seventeen full-time church members under our direction. We started as guests on a call-in talk show on a local radio station. On the show, we announced the topic of a public speech I would give, "Reverend Moon's Teachings and Their Contribution to Christianity." As we promoted the address, we created controversy.

On Wednesday, November 16, the day of the speech, a front-page article appeared in the local newspaper. At 11:20 a.m., protesters called in a bomb threat to the scheduled venue for the speech, an Econo Lodge. The management of the motel evacuated its guests. At 3:30 p.m., there was a second bomb threat, and everyone had to leave the building again. The callers insisted that we leave or they would detonate a bomb. In response, we rescheduled the event to take place in a nearby restaurant, where we met in one of their banquet rooms. The Associated Press got the story, and both the *Delaware State News* and the *News-Journal* of Wilmington showed up at the speech. Just before the program started, I called into a local talk show to express our resolve to carry on in spite of the threats from protesters. Under those circumstances, only four guests came.

Earlier in the day, a local rabbi had turned over our side-walk book table. He thought the Unification Church was anti-Semitic. During the speech, he and two local Christian ministers picketed the Econo Lodge. On the Saturday following the campaign, Mrs. Eu came to visit. She reminded us of Jesus' commandment to love your enemies and asked, "What are you doing to love the people who opposed you?"

I said, "We aren't doing anything."

She replied, "You know who opposed you. Go love them!"

With the intention of loving the protesters, we reached out to them. Unfortunately, we were unable to meet with them and address their concerns before we left for New Haven.

During the Dover campaign, my relationship with Mrs. Eu and my partnership with the state leader empowered me. In New Haven, I did not create a connection with the state leader or the Korean leader. I just went through the motions. Monday through Thursday we went street witnessing and met with local officials. On Friday and Saturday, we supported ourselves by selling flowers. I persevered without inspiration. At the end of twenty-one days, our leaders extended our stay in New Haven until January. After having uprooted ourselves five times, we were glad to remain in New Haven a little longer.

On December 22, 1983, tragedy struck. Heung Jin Moon, Reverend Moon's second son, sustained critical injuries in a car accident. He was part of my life. I had been with him at birthday celebrations in his home and at public events. He was devoted to his parents, and he was a champion of their purpose to establish God's kingdom on earth. After the crash, he remained in a coma until he died on January 2. His death left me grieving. My grief and my burnout daunted my enthusiasm, and I officially withdrew as a leader of a traveling team.

As an alternative, I accepted an assignment as an assistant to the state leader of Texas in Houston. I muddled through the days, trying to reconnect to a sense of purpose. When Reverend Won Pil Kim visited Houston, he saw I was struggling. He suggested I return to New York and work with Reverend Sudo at national headquarters. I took his advice and went back to New York.

Reverend Sudo welcomed me. He gave me the freedom to make my own schedule. I started seeing a therapist to regain my sense of well-being, and I went fundraising on weekends. As a result of individual and group therapy sessions, I dealt with my burnout. After two years of therapy, I was more in touch with myself and the world around me.

I also used this time of healing to take care of my health. I had been having digestive problems for more than a year, and my psychotherapist referred me to Connie, an alternative health specialist. Connie captivated me with her love for life, and we became great friends. She was a student of Joel Goldsmith, an American spiritual teacher. Curious about what he taught, I started reading his books and listening to his recordings. Joel described his work by saying, "Listen way down inside of yourself, and then remember that this day which lies ahead of you is now God-governed, God-protected, God-maintained, and God-sustained because you have consciously opened your consciousness to the presence and the government of God."[1] This mystical approach to divine empowerment resonated with me, and my spiritual life became informed more by Joel Goldsmith's precepts than by Reverend Moon's.

I transitioned to the fringe of the Unification Movement. I was living in a church center, but I was only peripherally engaged as a Unificationist. From time to time, I helped with the distribution of donated food, but I wasn't willing to stick with it. In an attempt to find something that I could do, Reverend Sudo asked me to track member information on a computer. I tried to figure out how to use the computer, but I gave up after only a few hours.

My lackluster participation affected my relationship with Reverend Moon. His teachings no longer appealed to me, and I stopped going to hear him speak. In the past, I had been through several trials of faith and revived. This time, my malaise lingered, and I wasn't receptive to offers of support.

After her graduation from the seminary, Amy became a CARP leader. When we saw each other, she expressed her annoyance that I wasn't accepting leadership responsibilities. She thought I was wasting my time with psychotherapy.

Based on my lack of interest in following Reverend Moon and participating in the Unification Church, Amy agreed to a divorce. I filed the paperwork, and our marriage officially ended. From the time of our matching in 1980 to the time we divorced in the spring of 1986, we did not consummate our marriage. Even though our relationship was more of an engagement than a marriage, I took it seriously, and I did not end it casually. For over a year, I had had my doubts about our future together.

When Amy and I chose to get a divorce, I informed Reverend Sudo that I was no longer a member of the Unification Church. I moved out of the church center and found a studio apartment. To pay the bills, I created a business selling aluminum foil prints.

Notes.

1.   Goldsmith, J. (1959). *A Lesson to Sam*. Marina Del Ray, CA: DeVorss.

CHAPTER 16

CHOOSING TO BE A LIBRARIAN

IN OCTOBER 1986, I was selling prints in Englewood, New Jersey, when I went into an Electrolux vacuum cleaner store. I talked with one of the employees, and she suggested I try selling vacuum cleaners. Within a few days, I relocated to New Jersey and attempted to sell vacuums. I worked hard for several weeks and sold nothing. Disappointed with my lack of success, I asked the repair manager if he needed any help. He said he did, and I moved from sales to service. I loved making repairs. As much as I enjoyed the work, it didn't pay well. To make ends meet, I divided my time between working in the service department and selling pictures.

Over the years, I sold thousands of small aluminum foil prints. One of the steady sellers was the poem, *Footprints*.[1] The words were superimposed on a picture of footprints on a sandy beach. People often recognized the poem, picked up the picture, and quietly read it. It describes a dream in which the Lord promises a man He will never leave him. In the dream, the man sees two sets of footprints on a beach. One set is his own, and the other is the Lord's. The man notices that in the most challenging times of his life, there is only one set of footprints. He asks the Lord why He left him when he needed Him most. The Lord replies, "It was then that I carried you."

Dozens of people told me stories of when they thought they had been abandoned by God only to find out later that He had always been with them. Sometimes it was a story of illness, sometimes the loss of a loved one, and sometimes a financial crisis. These little stories of God's abiding presence got me thinking about my own life. When I looked to see if He had been there in my times of trial, I saw that He had.

While I was going door-to-door selling my pictures at the beginning of 1987, I went into a bookstore. I picked up a book about adult children of alcoholics and leafed through it. As I was growing up, Dad drank a lot. He drank after work, and he drank when he got home. I never thought much about it. It was just the way it was. A comment in the book gave me a new viewpoint. It said that a person is an alcoholic if their use of alcohol impacts the quality of their relationships. There was no question about it. Dad's use of alcohol affected the quality of our family life. Based on this definition, I was an adult child of an alcoholic. This was a startling realization. I had never thought of Dad as an alcoholic, but it made sense. In the back of the book, I found a list of twelve-step meetings for adult children of alcoholics in New Jersey. I located one near me and began attending once a week.

By listening to other people sharing at these meetings, I became aware of the effect Dad's drinking had had on me. Because he was frequently under the influence of alcohol, I had learned that it wasn't safe to express my opinions and emotions around him. I had adapted by suppressing my self-expression. At the twelve-step meetings, I began to speak up and say what was in my heart and mind.

Then I learned about denial. People at the meetings told horrific stories about their experiences, yet often ended with "but it wasn't that bad." My internal reaction was, *"No, what you experienced was terrible!"* After a while, I could see I was doing the same thing they were doing. When I talked about what happened in our home, I ended with "but it wasn't that bad." At some point in the past, my denial had served to protect me from the pain in my life. It was time to face it. I needed to feel the heartache. As I let go of my claim that "it wasn't that bad," my heart softened, and I was able to heal.

What came next was a shock! Some of the people who told harrowing stories concluded that they were grateful for their experiences with their alcoholic parent. The first time I heard someone say this, I thought they were out of their mind. Then I heard other people say the same thing after telling about their trials. It absolutely made no sense to me. I could see no way to be grateful that Dad was short-tempered and emotionally distant.

Eventually, I was able to understand what they were talking about. They had claimed who they had become in life, and they were grateful for the experiences that had forged their character. They were celebrating their victory over their past. To me, they were heroic and inspiring. I thought about how I had adapted to the stress created by my father's alcoholism. I realized I had developed punctuality, self-discipline, a strong work ethic, and tolerance for irritable people. For the first time, I could appreciate who I had become as a person.

During this period of awakening, I started to wonder what I was going to do with the rest of my life. I was a capable, educated person, and I could do anything I wanted. In spite of my potential, all I was doing was getting by financially. One afternoon, as I was walking down the street on my way to my next sales approach, I stopped in my tracks. A new idea had interrupted my reflections on what was next. I could start a new career!

I went to the nearest pay phone and called the career counseling service at the Stevens Institute of Technology. A friend of mine had told me about their counseling service, and I decided to see what advice they could offer me. A few days later, I had the initial interview and took several aptitude tests. One of the tests was the Strong Interest Inventory. I had taken the same test at BYU in 1971. To my surprise, more than fifteen years later, the same career stood out as holding the greatest promise of satisfaction for me—librarian. I put my trust in the test results, made a commitment to discover the fulfillment waiting for me as a librarian, and applied to the Library School at Rutgers University.

Notes:

1. Carty, C. (2004). "Footprints in the Sand." Bloomington, IN: Author-House.

Chapter 17

A Match Made in Heaven

RUTGERS UNIVERSITY ACCEPTED my application, and in September 1987, I began taking classes in library science. From the very beginning, I loved it. My favorite part of the program was an internship as a cataloger of Romance language materials at Princeton University's Firestone Library. My high-school French and college Spanish were all I needed to work with books written in Latin-based languages. The staff in the cataloging department maintained the highest standards in creating cataloging records. When I finished my internship, I wanted to be a cataloger.

As I prepared for graduation from the library program, I started my job search. I even flew to Phoenix and interviewed at the Arizona State University library for a cataloging position. While I was looking for work, I got a call from my friend, Thomas Ward. Thomas was one of the directors of the American Leadership Conference funded by Reverend Moon and a product of the collaboration with Dr. Cleon Skousen. It held conference weekends all over the United States that provided political, religious, and community leaders with a faith-based alternative to communism. Thomas invited me to his office in Manhattan, and we set a time to meet.

We had not seen each other in more than a year, and we spent a few minutes reconnecting with each other. Thomas then offered me a job as the librarian for the American Leadership Conference. I was interested in the work of the organization; nevertheless, I wasn't ready to jump into a

Unification Church project. I had left my faith commitment to Reverend Moon and the Unification Church behind.

As I sat with Thomas in his office, I reflected on the ten years I had devoted to activities inspired by Reverend Moon. I told him I would not work for the American Leadership Conference unless I was a member of the Unification Church. To give the opportunity a chance, I told him that I would set a forty-day condition to pray and read the *Divine Principle*. Afterward, I would reconsider my faith commitment and his offer of employment.

In the course of those forty days, my attitude toward the Unification Church transformed. Initially, I did not find the *Divine Principle* uplifting. The words provided no spark of spiritual vitality. Part of my condition was to have a traditional Unification Church prayer service each Sunday morning at 5:00 a.m. and recite an affirmation of faith. At first, that statement of faith seemed foreign to me. As the days and weeks passed, I kept reading and praying.

After my prayer service one Sunday morning, I listened to some recordings of sermons I had given as a Unification Church leader. I was in total agreement with everything I said in those sermons, and I could see myself giving similar sermons again. As I reflected on the life I was living, what was missing was participation in a community of faith and a compelling purpose. Little by little, I revived my connection to the vision and hope I had had as a Unificationist.

By the end of the forty days, the *Divine Principle* had come alive, I had opened my heart to Reverend Moon, and I had embraced the affirmation of faith. I was ready to make a new beginning. I told Thomas I had decided to rejoin the Unification Church, and he again extended the offer to work with the American Leadership Conference. In August 1988, I began working as their librarian, and I resumed my life as an active member of the Unification Church. It was almost as if I had never left. There was no ceremony to re-establish my membership.

After I left the Unification Church, I remained single, and I maintained my sexual abstinence. When I returned, I invested myself in the work of the church with the intention of preparing myself to be a committed husband and father. Amy and I had not been in touch with each other during my absence. When I returned, I discovered that Reverend Moon had given her another match, which ruled out picking up where we left off.

Breaking Reverend Moon's Blessing of marriage was a serious matter. I would not qualify for another match for seven years. I was thirty-nine when I renewed my commitment to the Unification Church, and I determined that when I was forty-six, I would request to be matched again.

I devoted myself to the work of the Unification Church and to fulfilling my duties at the American Leadership Conference. I accepted the opportunity to serve as the church leader on the Rockaway Peninsula in Queens. As an extension of that responsibility, I actively engaged in interfaith work with clergy in various congregations throughout the borough. I also frequently preached on the street the message of the Unification Church, and I never missed a chance to attend Reverend Moon's speeches. Anytime he spoke in the New York area, I was there; attentive and eager to hear what he had to say.

My degree in library science got me started at the American Leadership Conference; however, before long, there was a need for a leasing agent for the public auditorium on the floor we occupied in our building. I assumed that responsibility and continued to serve as an information resource.

Dr. Bo Hi Pak was the leader of the American Leadership Conference. He was not present in the day-to-day operations, but he functioned as our liaison with Reverend Moon and authorized all of our activities. In November 1990, Dr. Pak invited me to lunch and asked me what I wanted to do with my life. It was a rare privilege to have personal time with him. He was one of Reverend Moon's closest associates. In my eyes, he was a spiritual giant and a man of great accomplishment. He asked if I had considered becoming a lawyer, a politician, or getting a PhD. He saw in me the potential to be a respected leader, and he was encouraging me to get the credentials that would enhance my credibility. I said him I had considered getting a PhD. He told me to enroll in a doctoral program and complete my degree as soon as possible.

In January 1991, I began my doctoral studies at Teachers College, Columbia University. I chose Teachers College because it was nearby, and they offered most of their courses in the late afternoon and evening. This allowed me to continue to work at the American Leadership Conference during the day. At first, I thought I would pursue a doctorate in the philosophy of education. After my first course, my professor told me I did not have a talent for philosophy. His assessment left me wondering what direction to take.

After completing my master's degree in sociology at BYU, I wanted nothing more to do with sociology as a discipline. Sociology does not study causal relationships. It only reveals what social variables are correlated with other social variables. I didn't think sociology generated useful findings. In an attempt to find a subject area for my doctorate, I took a course in the sociology of education. I thrived in the course. At BYU, I thought I did well in sociology because it was easy. I realized from the reactions of the other students in the class that it wasn't easy. I actually had a talent for it, and my academic background was a bonus. I gave up my concern about the limitations of sociology and accepted that the sociology of education could provide meaningful research to inform decisions about education. In the fall of 1991, I chose my advisers and created a plan to complete my doctoral program.

When I rejoined the Unification Church, Reverend Moon was emphasizing a return to our hometowns. Rather than move back to California, I found other ways to reach out to old friends. I subscribed to the *Oroville Mercury-Register* to stay in touch with what was going on where I had grown up. I also renewed old friendships by sending Christmas cards during the holidays. My Christmas card list included Miriam and her husband, David. Miriam and I grew up together in Oroville, and I knew her husband from BYU. Her mother, Emma Goddard, had suggested I go to BYU. Donna Bowers Harding and her husband, Terry, were also on the list. Michael, my former roommate and fraternity brother, and his wife, Tara, also got a card. They all responded, and we continued to exchange greetings every year. Without Reverend Moon's encouragement, I would not have revived those friendships.

In 1992, Reverend Moon set in motion the preparations for a major Blessing in August in Seoul, Korea. He planned to marry 30,000 couples—which meant he first needed to match the couples. Single members submitted a simple matching application with an eight-by-ten photograph. The application included their age, nationality, and education.

Since I had broken my Blessing with Amy, I presumed I was not eligible for this matching. Just in case, I asked a Korean leader if I qualified. He looked me straight in the eye and asked, "Are you committed to accepting Reverend Moon's match for you?"

"Yes," I affirmed.

"You are qualified," he asserted.

Having established my credentials, I submitted my application. I was virtually guaranteed a match. Many more women submitted applications than men. As a doctoral candidate and a graduate of the Unification Theological Seminary, I presumed my match would have a college degree. It was my understanding that Reverend Moon thought well-educated men should have well-educated wives. I wrote on my application that I preferred to be matched to a woman from Korea, Japan, or China. I had spent many years working with Asian Unificationists, and I wanted to have an Asian woman as my wife. Though I did not put it on the application, I prayed to have a spouse committed to having and raising children.

While waiting for this second matching, I learned several lessons about love and marriage from Reverend Moon. He depicted marriage as a pot of water. He said it is better to start a marriage with cold water in the pot rather than to start with the water boiling. Over time, love grows, and the pot comes to a boil. To prepare us for the matching, he had us imagine our match as our worst nightmare. I decided even if I had to sit in the car every night when I came home to get the courage to go into the house and deal with my worst nightmare, I would remain faithful and love her.

He also taught a concept called "winter love." It helped mature my understanding of love. In the winter, there is no external evidence of the wonders of spring. They are dormant. I realized I had been looking for a springtime love and ignoring the other seasons of love. I decided I would always acknowledge love is present and find joy in winter love, as well as spring, summer, and autumn love.

This quote from Reverend Moon depicts his approach to matching: "I have a philosophy of balance in matching—a harsh person needs to be balanced with someone soft. A weak, soft person needs someone strong. In machines, both hard and soft metals are needed to complement each other. People look only at the surface appearance in evaluating people, but a pretty woman and a handsome man together may lose everything and leave nothing behind. In matching people, I try to make a permanent base. I match from the viewpoint of central true love. Sometimes my methods look strange, or labyrinthine, and you can't see the light at the end of the tunnel. But if the end result will be true love, I will go that way."[1]

While I was submitting my application, a Brazilian woman living in the New York area was also preparing her application. Less than a year earlier, she had come to the United States to visit a relative. On the plane from Brazil, Alice Nohara sat with a woman who was a Unification Church member. She helped Alice find her way through the airport, and they stayed in touch after they arrived in New York. As an outgrowth of their friendship, Alice joined the Unification Church.

Alice had a bachelor's degree in nutrition and worked as a nutritionist and restaurant manager at a factory in São Paulo before coming to the United States. She was born in Brazil, and both her parents were from Okinawa, Japan. In her family, matching was a common practice. Her parents and grandparents were matched, and her father had even attempted to arrange a marriage partner for her. She had heard that when Reverend Moon matched couples, he discerned the compatibility of the ancestors of the couples. This appealed to Alice. She wanted a husband whose ancestors were aligned with hers. Though Alice did not put it on her application, she was looking for an intellectual man who would pray with her. She trusted God would give her the right husband.

Reverend Moon matched most of the 30,000 couples at his home in Kodiak, Alaska. To facilitate viewing the photos of the matching candidates, he had them arrayed in rows on stands similar to magazine racks. He had the pictures organized by characteristics such as education and nationality. For several days Reverend Moon prayerfully created couples from the images on display.

On Wednesday evening, July 15, 1992, at the national headquarters of the Unification Church in Manhattan, the matching announcement for members living in the New York area took place. There were several hundred of us gathered for the meeting. The person conducting the event called our names in alphabetical order by the last name of the men. Upon hearing his name, each man went to the front to accept his match with a bow. Sometimes the woman was not present. If not, the officiator told him where she was living. She might have been anywhere in the world.

When he called my name and announced Alice as my match, I heard voices in the crowd declaring: "She is here! She is here!" We went to the front of the room, bowed to accept our match, and went to the foyer to get acquainted. This was the first time we had ever seen each other. Immediately, I felt inner peace and joy in her presence. I prepared myself for the worst and received the best. I got a woman with Asian lineage who loved children, and she got an intellectual man to pray with. We saw the hand of God in our matching.

Alice was living in the national headquarters building as she participated in a forty-day training for new members of the Unification Church. I felt the fate of our relationship was in my hands. I looked for ways to win her heart. My office was just a few blocks away, and I stopped by every day to see her. Our visits were brief because she was busy with her training. On Sundays, I took her to hear Reverend Moon speak.

We could have participated in the Blessing in Korea remotely, but we both wanted to be there in person. Alice's visa had expired, and if we left the country to attend the Blessing, she would not be able to return to the United States until she obtained a green card. I counseled with Thomas Ward, and we came up with a plan. After going to the Blessing in Korea, Alice and I would proceed to Moscow, Russia, and stay there in an apartment maintained by the American Leadership Conference. After living in Russia for several months, we would go to Brazil and meet her family. Alice would then remain in Brazil until she received her green card, and I would return at the end of January to continue my studies. Alice agreed to the plan.

We consulted with an immigration lawyer, and he recommended that we get married and submit Alice's green card application before we left for Korea. We followed his advice, and we made our wedding vows in a civil ceremony in New York City on August 5, 1992. By the time we left for Korea two weeks later, I had tickets for us to go from Seoul, back to New York City, and on to Moscow.

Fortunately, I had the resources to make these travel arrangements. My mother's sister had died a year earlier with a living trust in place that I had set up for her when I worked with Connecticut General in the 1970s. At the time of her death, my brother Bert was serving as her trustee. He liquidated her estate and distributed the proceeds. Through my aunt's generosity, we had a memorable beginning to our marriage.

In the two weeks between the time of our marriage and our departure to Korea, I went to my twenty-fifth high school reunion in Oroville, California. When I graduated from high school, I left behind that troubled period in my life. If it had not been for Reverend Moon's emphasis on reconnecting with our hometowns, I would not have gone to the reunion. It turned out to be a healing experience. I walked right back into the lives of my classmates who I had not seen in decades and started fresh on the foundation of many shared memories from our youth. Alice was not able to attend because she was still completing her forty-day training; nevertheless, they acknowledged us as the most recently married.

When I returned to New York, Alice and I began our epic journey to Korea, Russia, and Brazil. In Seoul, we stayed at a site built for athletes in the Seoul Olympics with 1,500 other couples. The men slept in a large warehouse, lined up in rows on the floor. The women had more comfortable accommodations in bunk beds in another building. During our stay, Alice and I had a chance to get to know each other and fellowship with other couples in Korea for the Blessing.

On August 24, 1992, all the couples who had gone to Korea for the mass wedding gathered in the Seoul Olympic Stadium to prepare for the big event the next day. This was probably the largest wedding rehearsal in human history. On the day of the Blessing, as Alice and I walked to our seats from the stadium parking lot, we were in a sea of men in blue suits, white shirts, and red ties, and women in white wedding dresses and veils.

When the Blessing ceremony began, the brides and grooms filled the first level of the stadium, and some stood in rows on the field. There were 20,000 couples in the stadium and 10,000 more linked by satellite across the globe. The event began with the singing of Unification Church hymns, followed by Reverend Moon's prayer, and the repetition of our vows. With tens of thousands of other couples, we shared a sacred moment in which we dedicated our marriages to God and made a public statement of the importance of marriage and family. We then witnessed a stunning display of world-class entertainment. In a spontaneous expression of celebration, Alice and I joined in creating a human wave as it flowed around the stadium.

Several months earlier, a friend of mine, who was a Unification Church missionary in Africa, told me there were hundreds of couples in Zaire who could not afford to travel to Korea for the Blessing. To raise funds to send a few of those couples to Korea, I made an appeal in the *Unification Church News*. Thirty thousand dollars came in response to my notification, and I sent it to Zaire. After the Blessing, I received a letter of gratitude and learned that the money had not been used to send couples to Korea. It had been used to pay for a satellite link. All the matched couples in Zaire had participated in the Blessing. However, just because the Blessing was available in their own country did not mean it was easy to get to the location set up with a satellite link. A group of 30 Blessing candidates had left their homes two weeks in advance to be sure to be there on time and arrived one hour before the event began. What a thrill to find out the funds I had collected made it possible for hundreds of our brothers and sisters in faith to participate in the Blessing ceremony!

The day after the Blessing, the newlyweds went to see the sights in Seoul, including a Korean folk village. When Alice and I returned to New York, Alice stayed at the airport on a transit visa while I went to my apartment to get our winter clothes for our trip to Russia. Of all places, we were going to have a honeymoon in Moscow.

Notes:

1. Moon, S. (1980). "Liquidation and Blessing." New York: Holy Spirit Association for the Unification of World Christianity.

Chapter 18

To Russia with Love

WAITING TO GREET us at the airport in Moscow were loving Unification Church members whom we had never met. They drove us to our apartment and helped us adapt to our new surroundings. Our apartment building was a typical example of housing options. It was a six-floor walkup with three apartments on a floor. We shared a large, three-bedroom flat with one other Unificationist.

Russia was in an economic crisis. When Alice saw the living conditions in Moscow, she felt Brazil did not deserve a third-world designation. Many people were out of work, and many others worked without pay. It was common to see old women at subway stations selling a few withered vegetables they had grown in their gardens outside the city. People were financially desperate. There was a light fixture on the landing outside our apartment. There was no bulb in the socket. I replaced the bulb. Before long, the light bulb disappeared. I put another bulb in the socket. It disappeared again. I continued to put light bulbs in the socket until the light bulb needs of our floor were met, and one finally remained in place.

We learned to live like Russians. It took some time to learn how to shop for groceries. In the United States, we could just go to a supermarket, select what we wanted, take it to the check-out counter, and pay for everything in a single transaction. Not in Moscow. We had to go to several different stores and in each one, wait in one line to choose items and wait in another line to pay for them.

Near our apartment, there was a bread store, a vegetable store, and a meat and milk store. The bread store had delicious bread. Our favorite was a sourdough called borodinsky bread. Alice was in heaven with a cup of tea with milk and an assortment of different kinds of baked goods.

At the vegetable store, there were many root vegetables such as beets, turnips, carrots, and potatoes, and only a few aboveground vegetables such as tomatoes, cucumbers, celery, and leafy greens. At the meat and milk store, we discovered smetana, a milk product made from souring cream. I loved it. The whole process of going to several stores and waiting in lines became part of the cultural adventure.

In addition to the specialty stores, vendors sold food near the subway stations. They sold things that were not available at the government stores, like bananas and eggs. The food choices were limited, and we watched for opportunities to get something different. We never knew when a truck would arrive at a subway station, and the driver would get out and start selling things from the back. If we saw a line, we just got in it and bought whatever they were selling. Once I got in a line behind a truck, not knowing what was for sale, and ended up with an attractive, delicious cake.

Whether it was in the stores or at the subway stations, no one ever gave us a bag or anything to carry our purchases. The only exception was the egg vendors. They put eggs in a newspaper rolled into a cone. After a few weeks, I learned to take a bag with me whenever I left the apartment in case there was an opportunity to buy something.

One of the things we enjoyed in Moscow was going to the subway station near Moscow State University. There, we would set up a table with Unification Church literature in Russian and talk to people. One woman we met was an English teacher at the university, and we became good friends. She and her daughter came to our apartment, and we visited them in theirs. We also met university students who spoke English. We invited them over for dinner and gave them a lesson from the teachings of the Unification Church.

Alice is an extraordinary cook. One young man who came for dinner said Alice's cooking was the best food he had ever eaten in his life. She accepted his compliment, delighted that he enjoyed her cooking. She had the same limited choices of food that everyone else had—her secret was her talent for making things taste good.

Before long we were both taking language lessons. Erin, a Unificationist I had known for many years, was living in Moscow and working as an English teacher. Erin had a friend who taught Russian as a foreign language. Alice took English lessons from Erin, and I took Russian lessons from Erin's friend. Two days a week, we left our apartment early in the morning and traveled across the city for our language classes. In the afternoons, I practiced my Russian at our information table.

In December 1992, the American Leadership Conference sponsored a tour of Moscow for legislators from the United States. I served as part of the advance team to find accommodations. We decided on what the Russians call a *sanitorium* which is a resort-like place where people go to relax. The sanitorium we chose was on the outskirts of the city and had been used by the highest-level members of the communist party during the Soviet period. In 1992, it was all but deserted. There was an indoor swimming pool, a movie theater, and a large pool room. It was well maintained and a great place to stay.

As the time drew near for the tour, two staff members with the American Leadership Conference came to Moscow. To celebrate their arrival, we went to a Korean restaurant. The waiter seated us and gave us menus. When I placed my order, he told me, "We are out of that." I tried two more items on the menu, with the same response. I saw other people eating, and I said I would have what they had. The waiter said, "They got the last order." We were all ready for anything, so I said, "Just bring us something!" I had seen a couple at another table with a bottle of Pepsi, and I asked the waiter to bring us some Pepsi. He said, "We don't serve Pepsi. That couple brought their own." We settled for water. When the food came, it was filling, and it was a bargain. Dinner for four came to less than six US dollars.

We also took our friends to the only McDonald's restaurant in Moscow. It was a treat to have American food. Alice was surprised to see a mural of Rio de Janeiro, including the statue of Christ atop Corcovado Mountain, painted on the wall inside the restaurant. Throughout our stay in Moscow, Alice marveled at the beauty of the murals, sculptures, and paintings in public places like McDonald's and the subway stations.

When the legislators from the United States arrived for the tour, we shifted from living as natives to living as tourists. Moscow is a different world for a tourist. We went to the Bolshoi Ballet, the Moscow Circus, and a stunning ice-skating show. We visited the White House, which is the Russian seat of government, and the Gorbachev Institute. My favorite place was Sergei Posad, a center for the Russian Orthodox Church north of Moscow. It has been a revered pilgrimage site for centuries. Even though there were many buildings with beautiful medieval architecture, the sacred atmosphere left a greater impression on me than the beauty of the buildings.

Alice thought the day would never come when it was time to go to Brazil. She enjoyed the Russian people, who generously extended their kindness to us, but she wanted to see her family and go where it was warm. In mid-December, the time came. We again flew to New York City, and Alice waited at the airport as I exchanged our winter clothes for the summer clothes we would need in Brazil.

In Russia, we built our relationship with many little, shared experiences. We had grown together as husband and wife, and we were ready to go to Brazil.

Chapter 19

"He Is Better Than Japanese."

Alice wondered if her parents would accept me. They had their hearts set on their children having spouses with Japanese lineage. Even though two of her brothers had Brazilian spouses and her younger sister, Aurora's fiancé was a Brazilian, they still hoped Alice would find a Japanese husband. Aurora prepared them to accept me by telling them that I was a well-educated, religious man worthy of their daughter.

When we arrived, they greeted us warmly. At no point did her parents give any indication our marriage was less than what they had hoped for Alice. I was still cautious. Alice had told me that at the end of World War II, an American soldier had killed her paternal grandfather in the American invasion of Okinawa. I thought it might be hard for her father to have an American son-in-law.

One of the first things Alice and I did when we arrived at her parents' home was to pay our respects to her ancestors at their *buchidan*. Her parents observed the family-centered religious practices of their native Okinawa. A buchidan—literally "Buddha shelf"—is a cabinet kept in the home where a family honors their ancestors. There is no statue of Buddha; instead, there are tablets inscribed with the names of their ancestors. At this place of respect, they make offerings of incense, tea, water, and rice. On special occasions, they offer carefully prepared food and fresh flowers. Standing in front of this simple shrine, Alice and I each reverently lit a stick of incense and offered a silent prayer. I was glad to join Alice in this reverent acknowledgment of her ancestors.

Soon after we arrived in Brazil, we attended Aurora's wedding. Aurora married her high school sweetheart, Francisco. They had postponed the ceremony until Alice and I arrived. The reception gave Alice an opportunity to introduce me to her family. As I met one person after another, the embracing circle of her family became a reality to me.

During the preparations for the wedding, I could see the deep connection between Alice and her sister. Growing up, Alice had longed to have the companionship of a sister. Aurora's birth, when Alice was eight years old, fulfilled the desires of her heart, and throughout their lives, they have remained close.

The reception gave Alice's mother deep satisfaction. Aurora was the last of her children to marry, and now her job as a mother was complete. Surrounded by her children, their spouses and her extended family, she was supremely happy.

Within a week of our arrival in Brazil, I had the impression Alice was pregnant. When I told her that I thought she had conceived, she didn't think it was possible; nevertheless, she made an appointment with her gynecologist. Her doctor confirmed she was pregnant! Alice had left home in October 1991 to visit a relative in New York, and she had returned home married and expecting a child a little more than a year later. It was a dramatic change. When Alice had gone to the United States, she was in her late thirties, and there was some concern she might never marry.

Every morning, I picked up fresh bread at the store across the street, and later in the day, I took walks in the nearby park. In the process of getting out, I met their next-door neighbor, José. He was a single man in his late sixties who lived with his two single sisters. José sat by his window looking out over the sidewalk greeting passersby. He seemed to always be talking with someone. José spoke English, and we immediately became friends. We exchanged greetings and had extended conversations every day. Getting to know him helped me adapt to my surroundings.

Reverend Moon taught me how to love people. He said you have to serve people if you want to love them. He prodded us, "To love people, you have to do something for them like wash their socks, clean their toilet, or polish their shoes!" I looked for ways to serve Alice's relatives and win their hearts.

Alice's family owned a storefront grocery in the Ipiranga district in the city of São Paulo. Her father worked six days a week in the store with her mother's sister and brother. Obasan, her mother's sister, was the most resistant to family members marrying anyone who did not have Japanese lineage. I often visited the store to see if there was something I could do to help. Obasan remained aloof and seemed to only tolerate my presence.

One day, I saw her getting into their old Volkswagen van to go and pick up supplies, and she coolly accepted my offer to go along. When we arrived at the supermarket, I helped her load the shopping cart with sacks of beans, rice, and other commodities. At the checkout counter, she didn't have quite enough money to pay for everything, so I pulled out my wallet and gave her the money she needed. This small act of generosity melted her heart, and from that moment on, I could do no wrong. Obasan later confided in Alice that she had been angry I wasn't Japanese, but she had come to know I was a good man.

New Year's Day is a major holiday in the Brazilian-Japanese community. In preparation for this new beginning, the house is cleaned from top to bottom, everyone gets a haircut, and they make special food for the buchidan. Tradition dictates that on New Year's Day, all the members of the family visit the oldest son—in this case, my father-in-law. He would then reciprocate and go to their homes later in the day.

My wife's father was almost eighty-three, and he didn't drive anymore. In the afternoon, after all the relatives had come to pay their respects, he was ready to get in the van and visit them. He had hoped that Carlos, his oldest son, would drive. Since Carlos was busy with his wife's family, I filled in. Everywhere we went, his relatives welcomed us with beautifully prepared plates of traditional holiday food. They said, "Eat, eat! Try some!" Before long, I was very uncomfortable from overeating, but still, I did my best to honor their hospitality by sampling what they offered me. In spite of my discomfort, it was a pleasure to spend time with my father-in-law.

Alice's father and I had another memorable outing together toward the end of my six-week stay. José, their next-door neighbor, died unexpectedly. Alice's father had known José for many years and wanted to go to the funeral. We went together to pay our respects to our mutual friend.

I returned to the United States at the end of January 1993 for the spring semester at Columbia University, where I had two more years of PhD coursework to complete.

After I left Brazil, Alice's father told her I was a good man and added, "He is better than Japanese." This was the highest compliment he could have given me. I don't know what it was that touched him. It could have been going with him on New Year's Day to visit his relatives, our shared grieving at José's funeral, or making peace with Obasan. It meant even more to me because one of my countrymen had killed his father. This kind of resolution of historical resentments was part of Reverend Moon's vision for international and interracial marriage. I was proud to fulfill what I saw as part of God's purpose for our marriage.

I lived in a one-bedroom apartment on the third floor of a house near the beach in Rockaway Park in the New York City borough of Queens. Before we left for Korea, I had been renting out the bedroom and using the living room as a studio apartment for myself. My tenant had left, and I needed to get the bedroom ready for Alice. I painted it, had it carpeted, and put up new curtains. I transformed it into a beautiful room in honor of my bride.

At the beginning of March, Alice arrived from Brazil. She had never been to my apartment. When she walked in, she was shocked. She said, "You only have a black-and-white TV? And you don't even have a microwave?" With a modest beginning, we established our home, far from busy Manhattan.

Soon after we reunited in New York, Alice and I took a trip to California so that she could meet my relatives. My whole family warmly received her. Dad had remarried and his wife, Beverley, was a positive, loving presence in his life. Dad and Beverley put on a dinner for us and invited all our family members living in the San Francisco Bay Area. It was wonderful to have my family embrace Alice, accept us as a couple, and share our happiness that we would soon have a son.

On our trip to California, we visited people from my childhood in the spirit of Reverend Moon's direction to return to our hometowns. I intended to empower people I had known growing up with the vision and hope Reverend Moon inspired in me. With this intention, we visited Arlene, the wife of my boyhood scoutmaster. Her husband, Wally, was out of town, and we didn't have a chance to see him. Arlene told us they had joined the Church of Jesus Christ of Latter-day Saints. When I knew Wally and Arlene, they had been Baptists. I had no idea they had joined the Church. She said that in the early 1970s, Wally had a heart attack and was in the hospital for a prolonged recovery. Several times when she went to the hospital, she met a very kind man. His kindness in her time of need opened her heart and awakened her curiosity about his church. When Wally recovered, they both became Latter-day Saints.

Back in New York, it was soon time for Alice to give birth. What a joy to stand next to the doctor as he brought our son, David, into the world! Right after David took his first breath, the doctor handed him to me. Holding him for the first time gave me a feeling of fulfillment I had longed for. This was my son! What a sacred honor to be his father. Alice devoted herself to caring for him. In her love for David, I saw the answer to my prayer that my wife would find joy in being a parent.

I continued my doctoral studies and worked part-time as a librarian at the Manhattan Campus of Adelphi University. In 1994, Alice conceived again. To our delight, this time we had a girl. When it was time for Patricia's birth, there was no time to go to the hospital. She surprised us by coming sooner than we expected, and I had the great blessing of delivering Patricia at home in our apartment. What an intimate moment with my little girl!

Just before Patricia arrived in January 1995, I accepted a position as the library director at the Unification Theological Seminary. I started working at the seminary during the week and coming home on weekends. We waited to move closer to my work until Patricia was a month old. At the beginning of March 1995, we made the move and established our home in Kingston, New York, across the Hudson River from the seminary.

CHAPTER 20

A SHIFT IN PERSPECTIVE

IN 1983 I had confronted the public affairs director of the Church of Jesus Christ of Latter-day Saints with the limitations of their welfare program. I was expressing one of my justifications for keeping my distance. I thought there was a gap between the truth the Church taught and its actual practices.

My understanding of the Church's welfare program changed one day in the late 1990s. I was having lunch with a friend in the Unification Theological Seminary dining hall, surrounded by students and faculty members. My friend was the director of the International Relief Friendship Foundation, the relief organization of the Unification Movement.

When I inquired about the foundation's relief work, my friend said, "Here is something that might interest you because of your background with the Mormons. There is a famine in North Korea, and many aid organizations have tried to get food into the country. Only one aid organization has been successful. All the others have put restrictions on their offers of food, such as requiring that it be given only to civilians. They would not accept our offer of aid because we required someone to accompany the delivery. The North Koreans rejected all offers of aid with any restrictions."

She then told me, "The only organization that has been able to get food into North Korea is the Church of Jesus Christ of Latter-day Saints. They put no strings on their donation of food. It could be used to feed anyone, and they did not require a representative to accompany the delivery."

This expression of generosity touched my heart. Reverend Moon was from North Korea, and I had a deep concern for the welfare of the people in his homeland. This magnanimous gift of food dissolved one of my barriers to taking the Church seriously. This was evidence to me that Latter-day Saints were genuinely concerned about the poor.

As a seminary librarian with a background in sociology, I read the academic literature on new religious movements. An article by a prominent scholar in the Sociology of Religion caught my attention. In an essay entitled "The Rise of a New World Faith,"[1] he made a case for the Church of Jesus Christ of Latter-day Saints becoming the first new world faith since Islam. In my mind, the Church was a regional religion with a membership primarily in the western United States. It surprised me to read this scholar's opinion that the Church was becoming a significant new religious tradition.

Shortly after reading this essay, I learned that the member-ship of the Church of Jesus Christ of Latter-day Saints in other countries had surpassed the number of members in the United States. This expansion in membership and the essay on the Church as an emerging world faith shifted my viewpoint. I could no longer think of it as a minor North American religious movement.

The same Sociology of Religion scholar observed that the growth rate of early Christianity and the growth rate of the Church of Jesus Christ of Latter-day Saints are similar.[2] I carefully examined his graph depicting these parallel increases in membership. While I looked at the graph, I remembered the testimonies of Latter-day Saints who professed that their church was the restoration of first-century Christianity. The similarity in growth rates served as evidence to me that those testimonies were valid. I had a quiet assurance that Christ's church had been restored.

Even though my perception of the Church of Jesus Christ of Latter-day Saints expanded, my new view had no observable effect. It certainly didn't prompt me to consider becoming a member. My attention was on my duties as a library director and on my ministry with the Unification Church.

As I found fulfillment in the many demands on my time, I neglected my dissertation. In the fall of 1997, I overheard the president of the seminary finding fault with someone who had not finished his dissertation. His comments stirred my sense of pride. I felt that I had to achieve my goal of getting a PhD or people would one day gossip about what I had not accomplished. I put completing my thesis as my priority and worked intensively for five months. In the spring of 1998, it was done!

When we moved to Kingston in 1995, I called the bishop of the Kingston Ward to get the number of my old friend, Carl Markle. At that time, Carl worked as a salesman in a bed store near our home. We renewed our friendship, and I often visited him at his store after work. Through these visits, he became a trusted confidant.

Whenever I went to see him, he would ask, "So what's new?" I openly shared with him whatever was coming up in my life, and he kept me informed about activities at the Kingston Ward. For four years, my wife and I and our two children attended church meetings and activities at his invitation. Alice loved the welcoming handshakes and the warm embraces the ward members freely extended to us. One time, Carl invited us to the ward chili cook-off. Alice had never made chili before, and she gave it a try. People loved her chili, and they touched her heart with their compliments.

About the time I completed my dissertation, Carl invited me to hear the president of the Church of Jesus Christ of Latter-day Saints, Gordon B. Hinckley, speak at Madison Square Garden. This was a rare opportunity to be with President Hinckley. I saw it as an opportunity for interfaith fellowship. I accepted Carl's invitation, and I took Alice, David, and Patricia with me.

The cultural and racial diversity of the attendees impressed me. To meet the needs of the audience, interpreters made the proceedings available in eleven languages. This was definitely a faith with a broad appeal. With 24,000 people in attendance, it was the largest event in New York City ever sponsored by the Church. In spite of the size of the audience, there was a feeling of intimacy.

President Hinckley spoke with conviction, power, and authority. At eighty-seven years of age, he demonstrated he was fully capable of leading a church with millions of members. President Hinckley impressed me with the loving care he extended to his wife Marjorie, who accompanied him. He made sure she was seated first and tenderly held her arm as they walked together.

Less than two months later in June, my wife and I were in Madison Square Garden for a Unification Church event. By satellite, people all over the world participated in a Unification Church Blessing ceremony officiated by Reverend Moon and his wife. Before the Blessing, there was a pro-family rally with video depictions of several of the world's religions including Hinduism, Buddhism, Judaism, Christianity, Sikhism, and Islam. From the podium, leaders from those various religions affirmed the value of marriage.

Carl came with us to watch our children so Alice and I could participate. We were among the hundreds of couples lined up on the floor of Madison Square Garden to rededicate their marriages and receive the Blessing of marriage from Reverend and Mrs. Moon. It was thrilling to be part of this powerful, interfaith declaration of the value of marriage and family.

These two events were both inspiring, yet very different. The meeting with President Hinckley was an affirmation of faith. As an expression of their faith, the congregation acknowledged President Hinckley's leadership by singing "We Thank Thee, O God, for a Prophet."[3] When President Hinckley spoke, he praised those Latter-day Saints for their faithfulness in living the gospel and provided them with loving counsel.

In contrast, the meeting with Reverend Moon was a pioneering and visionary convergence of religions, focused on the importance of marriage and family. President Hinckley moved me by the embracing way he extended himself to the assembly, and Reverend Moon inspired me with his bold stand for unity among the world's religions. The most lasting impact on me from the two events was President Hinckley's pastoral care.

In June 1998, my family joined me in celebrating the completion of my doctoral program. I saw my accomplishment as an opportunity to share with BYU alumni. I submitted to the alumni magazine an announcement that I had received a PhD in education from Columbia University, and I was the library director at the Unification Theological Seminary. It was my way of publicly declaring I was a follower of Reverend Moon. My announcement appeared in the section devoted to alumni news. With my published notice, I included the graduates of my alma mater in what was important to me.

In the early 1990s, I bought a duplex in Hackensack, New Jersey, as a rental property. The tenants on the first floor were often unhappy with the renters upstairs. When the second-floor tenants moved out in June 1998, I asked the first-floor tenants if they wanted to choose their new neighbors. They were glad to do so and met with prospects. They made their choice, and to my surprise, I started receiving rent checks from the Church of Jesus Christ of Latter-day Saints. The first-floor tenants had rented the second floor to the Church to provide housing for full-time missionaries!

When I went to mow the lawn, I greeted the missionaries living there. We had brief conversations, and I was left wanting more. I admired them for their faith and spiritual vitality. If they had asked to teach me, I would have accepted just so I could spend more time with them. However, I said nothing to indicate I was interested in the gospel, and our conversations remained sporadic and superficial.

A few months later, Carl invited my family and me to attend a special meeting to hear President Ronald A. Rasband, the local mission president, speak. His comment on missionary work impressed me. He said the most effective way to support people interested in the Church was to host them in your home and have the missionaries teach them there. I had spent years street witnessing, street preaching, and knocking on doors to share with people the Unification Church message. I was in total agreement with President Rasband. I decided to use his strategy to serve my own purpose. I began to look for an opportunity to invite members of the Church of Jesus Christ of Latter-day Saints to our home to teach them about the Unification Church.

In December 1998, I went to Korea to attend a workshop and to visit the Korean counterpart of the Unification Theological Seminary. I expected to return spiritually nourished. Quite the opposite, I returned spiritually drained.

My first Sunday back, I went to the Kingston Ward with my family. A deep feeling of love came over me during the opening hymn, and tears poured from my eyes. During the talks, I wept again. Throughout the three hours of church meetings, I frequently broke into tears. I had never felt such an outpouring of the love of God and such comfort to my soul.

The next day, a Unification Church evangelist came to the seminary and initiated a witnessing campaign. For several weeks, I fully engaged in sharing Reverend Moon's vision of hope for individuals, families and the world. Focusing on our outreach obscured the impact of the love I had felt during the Kingston Ward meetings. Even with that profound experience of being loved, I remained committed to the Unification Church.

Notes:

1. Stark, R. (1998). "The Rise of a New World Faith." In *Latter-day Saint Social Life: Social Research on the LDS Church and its Members*. Provo, UT: Religious Studies Center, Brigham Young University, 1-8.

2. Stark, R. (1996). *The Rise of Christianity*. San Francisco: Princeton University Press.

3. Fowler, W. (1863). "We Thank Thee, O God, for a Prophet." In *Hymns of The Church of Jesus Christ of Latter-day Saints*, 1985. Salt Lake City, Utah: The Church of Jesus Christ of Latter-day Saints.

CHAPTER 21

HONOR YOUR FATHER AND YOUR MOTHER[1]

ALICE'S FAMILY EMIGRATED from Okinawa, Japan, to Brazil in the 1920s. Despite becoming Catholic as part of their assimilation into Brazilian culture, her family maintained the tradition of praying to their ancestors. Alice grew up praying to both God and to family members who had passed on. In the back of her mind, she was looking for a way to harmonize these two expressions of piety.

In January 1999, while Alice and I were at the supermarket, I noticed two missionaries from the Church of Jesus Christ of Latter-day Saints. We initiated a conversation, and we learned that one of the missionaries, Elder Yuba, was from Japan. This was the first time we had ever met a Japanese Latter-day Saint on a mission. By the time we ended the conversation, they had accepted an invitation to come to our home for dinner.

Alice and I both looked forward to their visit. Alice wanted to get to know Elder Yuba, and I was eager to introduce those missionaries to the Unification Church.

I invited a young Japanese couple who were students at the seminary to come to dinner as well. The wife, Satoko, had had a challenging and inspiring trial of faith. She had joined the Unification Church in spite of her parents' disapproval. Later, her parents hired abductors to remove her from the Unification Church in Japan, and she succeeded in a daring escape from her captors. She was a heroine among Unification Church members. I planned to have Satoko tell her story and impress the missionaries with her faith-based courage and conviction.

The day of our interfaith meeting arrived. Elder Yuba and his companion, the Japanese couple, and Jim Harris, a Latter-day Saint friend, joined us for dinner. I had invited Jim to add balance and depth to our dinner conversation. We started our evening listening to Satoko play the piano. She was an accomplished pianist, and her music created a welcoming atmosphere.

We enjoyed a casual conversation as we shared the meal Alice had lovingly prepared. Just before dessert, I asked Elder Yuba to tell us how he had joined the Church. With confidence, he told us his story.

"The first missionaries I met were in Japan teaching English, and we became friends as I studied with them. I wanted to get to know them better, and I asked them to teach me about their church. As they did, I felt its truthfulness."

We listened intently as Elder Yuba looked each of us in the eye and told us how much he had wanted to join the Church. However, he was concerned his parents would not approve. Instead of running the risk of offending them, he decided to wait.

Knowing he was interested in learning English, the missionaries suggested he apply to Ricks College in Idaho, a college funded by the Church of Jesus Christ of Latter-day Saints. The college accepted his application, and he went to Idaho to pursue his education. During his first semester, he continued to study the gospel and strengthen his conviction to become a Latter-day Saint. A few months later, he asked his parents for their approval. They granted him permission, and with their blessing, he made his baptismal covenant with the Lord.

His testimony shifted the course of the evening. He stunned the Japanese couple, Alice, and me with his story. He had respected his parents and maintained his close relationship with them during the process of his conversion. As much as Satoko had an inspiring story that demonstrated her faith commitment, it was also a story of family breakdown and ongoing ill will. I abandoned my plan to have Satoko share her triumph of faith.

When Elder Yuba finished, Alice said, "You told us you are the eldest son in your family. As the eldest son in a Japanese family, you have an obligation to pray to your ancestors. How do you fulfill your duty to pray to your ancestors and to pray to God?"

Elder Yuba responded, "I pray to God, and I pray *for* my ancestors." His simple answer resolved an unspoken concern that had been on Alice's mind most of her life. His explanation shifted her relationship with her ancestors. She went from appealing to them for help to asking God to bless them. With this new sense of order, she found clarity, comfort, and peace. From then on, Alice followed his example and prayed to God, and *for* her ancestors.

This dinner was a turning point for Alice. Even though we had attended many meetings with Latter-day Saints, she had never been interested in learning more about the Church. Elder Yuba opened her heart. When everyone had left, she told me she wanted our children to be like him and his companion—self-assured, polite, and respectful.

When Jim Harris arrived that night, he gave me a copy of a book he had edited on the writings of Elder James Talmage, entitled *The Essential James E. Talmage.* I had great respect for Elder Talmage, who had been an influential leader of the Church of Jesus Christ of Latter-day Saints, and I had enjoyed reading his book, *Jesus the Christ,*[2] while I was at BYU. Jim's book about Elder Talmage's life and work piqued my interest. From time to time, I read a few pages. I particularly enjoyed the story of Elder Talmage's baptism.

In 1873, when Elder Talmage was eleven, he fell ill. "His father blamed this on his not having yet been baptized. His baptism had been postponed because the opposition to the church was so strong in the area. When James had recovered, he and two of his friends were to enter the water the same evening, the baptism being held at night as not to arouse local hostilities. As James stepped to the water's edge, they reportedly heard a terrible shriek, which James described as 'A combination of every fiendish ejaculation you could think of.' His father asked if he wanted to proceed, and James said yes. The noise stopped the moment he stepped into the water."[3]

In the course of my life of faith, I had observed spiritual opposition similar to the opposition surrounding Elder Talmage's baptism. I read the account again and again. I could imagine his father interpreting his illness as an indication he was not under God's protection. He impressed me with his courage to be baptized under those circumstances.

Our dinner meeting drew both Alice and me closer to the Church. Alice saw that she could pray *for* her ancestors and pray to God, and she was left wanting our children to be like those missionaries. Jim Harris' book opened my heart to the gospel as I reflected on the life and teachings of Elder Talmage.

Notes:

1. Exodus 20:12.

2. Talmage, J. (1915). *Jesus the Christ: A Study of the Messiah and His Mission According to the Holy Scriptures Both Ancient and Modern*. Deseret Book: Salt Lake City, Utah.

3. Harris, J. (Ed.). (1997). *The Essential James E. Talmage*. Signature Books: Salt Lake City, Utah.

CHAPTER 22

SPIRITUAL DISCONTENT

IN JANUARY 1999, the same month Alice and I had our memorable dinner with Elder Yuba, I called my friend Thomas Ward. I told him I was looking for a change, and I was considering leaving the seminary. Thomas suggested we get together for a prayer vigil. It was a custom in the Unification Church to have periodic prayer vigils from midnight to four in the morning. Thomas and I met at his house in Poughkeepsie, New York, and for four hours we prayed, sang hymns, and studied Reverend Moon's speeches. In parting, Thomas suggested I stay on at the seminary for the time being and fully engage in Unification Church activities. I accepted his suggestion and put aside my thoughts of looking for another job.

In February, I joined the preparations for an event in April. Reverend Moon's wife was going to speak in Poughkeepsie. I accepted a leadership role in scheduling entertainment, inviting community leaders, and encouraging local Unificationists to ask their friends to come to the speech. Even though the event was well attended, I found no joy in our accomplishment. I was just glad it was over.

Later in April, a Korean leader came to the United States to conduct ancestor liberations for Unification Church members. Alice and I submitted the names of some of our ancestors and participated in the liberation ceremony. The purpose of ancestor liberation was to release our kindred dead from any attachments to the physical world. Many of my friends found the ceremony empowering; however, I couldn't see the value of it.

In June, I went to Korea with other Unificationists from the United States to attend a special event sponsored by Reverend Moon and spent a week in Seoul. We heard Reverend Moon speak in the intimate surroundings of his home, as well as at a major public event. I had thought going to Korea would result in having a deeper connection to Reverend Moon. That did not happen. I left Korea frustrated that I did not find the spiritual empowerment I was looking for.

Right after I returned to the United States, Alice and I took our children with us to Brazil for a forty-day training at a Unification Church workshop. There were five hundred Unification Church members in attendance from all over the world. Our primary activity was listening to someone read Reverend Moon's speeches. We also sang songs, shared inspiring stories, and provided service around the workshop site. While we were there, Reverend Moon was on a fishing trip nearby on the Paraguay River, and many of us took a boat trip up the river to meet with him. I loved sitting with Reverend Moon beside the river as he imparted his guidance to us.

The forty-day training introduced me to various economic and educational enterprises Reverend Moon had begun in Brazil. I even considered making a long-term commitment to those projects. Back in the United States, I chose not to participate in those activities. In familiar surroundings and with the excitement of the workshop far away, I had a different perspective. One of the projects was driven by a plan to establish a lumber business in Brazil by growing eucalyptus trees, but no one knew much about the market for eucalyptus wood. Another project was to establish a school, but those in charge had overlooked the environmental impact of the building they had erected, and they were out of touch with the needs of the faculty. In my opinion, there was not enough thoughtful planning.

Of all the Unification Church activities I was part of in 1999, my greatest hope for finding personal fulfillment was in a Blessing ceremony for our ancestors. From my viewpoint, the Blessing extended by Reverend Moon and his wife to unite couples centered on God constituted a sacred outpouring of God's love. On September 5 at the Manhattan Center, Alice and I participated as proxies in a Blessing ceremony for our ancestors. We joined with hundreds of other Unification Church couples who also served as proxies for their ancestors.

My expectations were high. This was the first time the Blessing was available to our kindred dead. Through this ceremony, we would be able to contribute to their spiritual progress. I anticipated that it would have the same effect on me as temple service had on my friends who were Latter-day Saints.

The Blessing ceremony was anticlimactic. I did not get the sense of freedom, hope, and comfort I expected. My disappointment undermined my confidence in the Blessing ceremony as a way to uplift my ancestors.

When I had returned to the Unification Church in 1988, I had started reading the *Divine Principle* as a daily source of spiritual nourishment. I had a vague sense that it was the definitive expression of the fundamentals of my faith. Joseph Smith said the Book of Mormon is "the keystone of our religion."[1] I presumed that similarly, the *Divine Principle* constituted the basis for the Unification Church.

In 1994, I was with Reverend Moon at his home in Irvington, New York, when he announced he was initiating a new translation of the *Divine Principle* into English. He described how he and Hyo Won Eu had worked together to write the book, but stopped short of declaring it as the primary point of reference for his teachings. As a result, I started to doubt my understanding of what he taught.

Not long after launching the new translation, he initiated the translation of all the speeches he had ever given into English. He directed us to read those speeches as a way to understand his heart and mind. His early speeches were given exclusively to Korean audiences, and I was unable to sift through the cultural references to come away inspired. So, I kept reading the *Divine Principle* as my way of connecting to the vision, which gave me the conviction to carry on.

However, after the Blessing ceremony for my ancestors, reading the *Divine Principle* did not feed my soul as it had in the past. One day in October 1999, I took a lunch break and drove to a park near the seminary to quietly sit and read the *Divine Principle*. I felt nothing—no hint of inspiration, no glimmer of hope. In my despair, I broke down and wept. I felt like I was spiritually starving.

At the end of October, Reverend and Mrs. Moon lost another son, Young Jin. He died in a tragic accident. I had known Young Jin since he was a boy. The last time I had seen him was when I was completing my doctorate. At the time, he was also a student at Columbia University. We ran into each other on campus, and we had a brief conversation. He was an outstanding young man in his own right, and he had the added advantage of the spiritual heritage of his inspired parents. He gave me hope for the future of Unificationism. I grieved his loss.

After almost a year of intense activities, I was spiritually discontent. I was actively participating in the Unification Church without a sense of connection to the value of our work. In this state of frustration, I confided in Carl. He listened to me as I described what I was going through, and he gave me the comfort of being heard.

Notes:

1. Smith, J. (1981). "Introduction." *Book of Mormon*. Salt Lake City, Utah: The Church of Jesus Christ of Latter-day Saints.

CHAPTER 23

THEOLOGICAL PING-PONG

A FEW MONTHS after our dinner with Elder Yuba and his companion, Reverend Moon directed seminary graduates to connect to other churches—not just once a month or once a week, but daily. As usual, Reverend Moon challenged us to stretch ourselves. I determined to make an even greater effort to build relationships with Latter-day Saints, and I began attending the Kingston Ward with my family as often as I could.

In August 1999, the bishop's wife organized a Joy School. Parents organize and teach this preschool program. It is intended to prepare children socially and emotionally for academic learning. Bishop Avenius asked his wife to see if Alice would be interested in joining the school with our daughter. Alice welcomed the opportunity, and soon she was actively participating in the classes with Patricia.

After they had been meeting for several weeks, Sister Avenius told Alice that the children in the Kingston Ward were going to lead a Sunday worship service. Alice wanted to go. She was a helper in the Sunday School for children at the Unification Church and wanted to see what Latter-day Saints provided for their young people. She arranged to have someone cover for her at the Unification Church, and she took Patricia and David with her to the presentation. I had obligations at the seminary church service, and I was not able to join them until noon.

When I arrived, the children's presentation was over, and it was the beginning of the third hour of church meetings.

I asked Alice if she wanted to stay and she said she did. Alice went to Relief Society, David and Patricia remained in Sunday School, and I met with the Elders Quorum.

In the Elders Quorum meeting, the quorum president encouraged the men to do their home teaching. Home teaching was the practice of Latter-day Saints teaching and serving member families. As a church leader in the Unification Church, I knew the value of home visits. At the training in Brazil the previous summer, a Korean leader had moved me with his accounts of visits with members in their homes. Even though I understood the value of being with members in their homes, I only made occasional visits to Unification Church members. The quorum president's advocacy for home teaching left me wanting to join them in their visits to Kingston Ward members.

After church, my friend Jim Harris introduced me to a visiting church leader. Although we merely greeted each other casually, he impressed me with his spiritual clarity and empowering presence. Later, I was in the parking lot as he drove away. As I watched him go down the road, I wondered what made him different from other men. I wanted what he had.

That church leader reminded me of a bishop at BYU. As he presided over church meetings, he conveyed the reality of the loving presence of Jesus Christ. I attributed his warmth to him as a person. Two years later when he was no longer leading a congregation, I saw him in the university library. When I greeted him, I asked him what he was doing. He explained he was completing an advanced degree. In our conversation, I did not feel the same loving presence I had felt when he was a bishop. I concluded that the quality I had attributed to him as a person was actually God working through him in his leadership position. I wondered if what I felt with the church leader visiting the Kingston Ward was also associated with his service on behalf of God.

After the meetings ended, Bishop Avenius invited us to have lunch with his family. We accepted and drove to the

Avenius' home. As I stood beside Bishop Avenius while he barbecued the meat, we had time to talk. He was a man with many interests and had much to say, but he still gave me a chance to talk about myself. It was great to have him take a personal interest in me. When I told him about going to BYU, he mentioned that Sister Avenius had attended BYU while I was there. He added that she was not a member at the time either.

Over lunch, I learned Sister Avenius had wanted to join the Church when she was a student at BYU, but her parents were unsupportive. Out of respect for them, she waited to make her baptismal covenant until after she graduated. Our shared experience as non-members at BYU created a foundation of trust between us.

At the dinner table, I sat next to Bishop Avenius, and we talked about the doctrines of the Church. He was a man who got to the point quickly. After hearing my responses on a few doctrinal topics, he spoke to me directly. "Brother Bowers, I am never going to talk with you about church doctrine again. All you want to do is play theological ping-pong. I state a point of doctrine, and you give it right back to me with your own understanding, without giving any consideration to what I have said."

He took me by surprise. Humbled and shocked by his insight, I knew he was right. He had called me on my game. I had been playing theological ping-pong with Latter-day Saints since the first missionaries taught me in 1969.

Over the years, I had many discussions with Latter-day Saints about their church's doctrines, but the format of the discussions was always the same. They would say what they believed, and I would say what I believed, back and forth. I had never identified it as a game. Bishop Avenius cut through my pretense of interest in the Church and exposed the way I kept my distance. I was responding to points of doctrine as if they were volleys in a game to be skillfully returned.

As I processed Bishop Avenius' observation, Alice said she thought it was good to have the children actively participate in a worship service. She also expressed her appreciation for the way they supervised the children's Sunday School. Alice wanted the best for David and Patricia, and she began to think the Sunday School program at the Kingston Ward would be a good way for them to learn about God and Jesus Christ. Some of my friends had accepted the challenge to create a meaningful children's curriculum for the Unification Church. While they had made progress, both my wife and I wanted more than the Sunday School program at the Unification Church had to offer.

Overall, we had a good visit with the bishop and his family. Bishop Avenius and I discovered we had many common interests, and we enjoyed each other's company. I bonded with Sister Avenius because we had been at BYU as non-members at the same time, and Sister Avenius impressed Alice with her warmth and friendship. We would inevitably see each other again, and when we did, I would not play theological ping-pong. By exposing my game, Bishop Avenius ended it and opened the way for me to take the Church's message seriously.

CHAPTER 24

THAT IS THE SPIRIT

THE SAME MONTH we met with the Avenius family, a young Latter-day Saint, Elder Stokes, arrived in the Kingston Ward as a missionary. My friend Carl had him over for dinner and gave him my name and number. When he gave Elder Stokes my contact information, he added, "He is ready." Carl had been waiting for the right time to send the missionaries to me, and he thought this was it.

Elder Stokes had been praying to meet a prepared family he could teach and baptize. He received my name as an answer to his prayers. When he told his companion about the referral, he responded, "I've been to his home for dinner, and he is filled with his own ideas. There is no point in trying to teach him." Elder Stokes decided he would find a time to meet with me when his new companion arrived in a few weeks.

As Elder Stokes bided his time, one night he heard a distinct voice say, "Call Tom Bowers." He had just come home after a day of missionary work and pushed aside the prompting. Before long he heard again, "Call Tom Bowers." He still did not pick up the phone. Finally, he heard, "Call Tom Bowers, now!" He then dialed my number.

I answered and asked bluntly, "Why are you calling me?"

"Carl Markle gave me your name," Elder Stokes explained. "But I'm calling you right now because the Spirit prompted me to do so."

He spoke with authority and conviction, and I took him at his word. We agreed to find a time to meet after my family and I returned from a trip to California.

As soon as I hung up with Elder Stokes, the phone rang again. The dean of the College of Theology at Sun Moon University was calling to request a copy of an early manuscript of Reverend Moon's writings we had in the seminary library. This was not routine. I had never before received a phone call from Korea regarding any library business. Afterward, I had the impression that Elder Stokes had been guided to call me before the call from Korea came. Receiving a call from him first seemed to serve a divine purpose.

After our California trip, I called Elder Stokes, and we set a time for him to come over for dinner. I didn't expect our meeting to be any different from past dinners with missionaries. When they arrived, Elder Stokes was clearly in charge. His companion, Elder Bundy, had just come from the missionary training center in Utah. Elder Stokes set the tone with an embracing attitude and a smile that lit up the room. He dutifully wore the suit and tie of a full-time missionary for the Church of Jesus Christ of Latter-day Saints, but his manner suggested he preferred more casual clothes. I could see him playing sports and enjoying the outdoors. I quickly discovered that even though he liked to tease, he knew when to be serious.

After the meal and a cordial conversation, Elder Stokes handed me his scriptures and asked, "Tom, would you read a passage from Galatians?"

"Sure!" I said, happy to have the Bible as common ground. He pointed to the verses he wanted me to read: Galatians 5:22-23. From the worn pages of his scriptures, I read aloud, "But the fruit of the Spirit is love, joy, peace, longsuffering, gentleness, goodness, faith, meekness, temperance: against such there is no law." It was a familiar passage, yet his next question had me pause.

"Tom, how does that make you feel?"

Initially, I wasn't aware of feeling anything. I wanted to respond sincerely, and I had nothing to say. In an attempt to be honest and direct, I said, "Good."

Without hesitation, he said, "That is the Spirit."

Surprised, I responded, "You mean that is the Spirit? This hardly noticeable good feeling?"

He said, "Yes."

I replied, "Elder Stokes, I have been around Mormons on and off for many years. I have often heard them talk about feeling the Spirit. Until now, my idea has been that the Spirit is one of the three beings that constitute the nature of God. It was just a concept. Now, I know for myself what it's like to feel the Spirit. Thank you!"

With this positive response to reading the scriptures, Elder Stokes leaned forward and asked, "May Elder Bundy and I teach you and your wife the gospel?"

This was a first. None of the missionaries who had been in our home over the years had ever asked to teach us. I responded, "We have our own religion, and we don't want to join the Mormon Church."

Elder Stokes persisted, "In just a few minutes of prayerful discussion, you came to know what it's like to feel the Spirit. The Lord has many more things to reveal to you. Will you let us teach you?"

I hedged, "Elder Stokes, I enjoy your company. However, I am only willing to let you teach us if we can approach our discussions as a faith-promoting experience for both of us rather than a pathway to conversion for my family and me."

Elder Stokes said, "Agreed."

Alice also accepted their request to teach us. We scheduled a time for their next visit, and they were on their way. Every time they came, they had dinner with us and taught us a lesson. They remained confident we would be baptized; however, I didn't think Alice and I were good prospects.

When Elder Stokes and Elder Bundy met with Bishop Avenius the following Sunday, they told him they were teaching us.

Bishop Avenius said, "You are wasting your time!"

Elder Stokes declared, "You are the bishop, and we are the missionaries. We will teach anyone we want!" When Elder

Stokes related the incident to me, I felt his commitment to preach the gospel, and I liked his boldness with the bishop.

Before the missionaries came again, I reflected on Elder Stokes' simple assertion, "That is the Spirit." I had only discerned the Spirit because he had pointed it out. It occurred to me that I must have felt the Spirit many times before and I didn't know it. While pondering when I might have felt the Spirit in the past, I remembered moments that made no sense at the time.

As a student at Brigham Young University, I had often felt a warmth in my heart, which left a smile on my face. A student had once come up to me and said, "A penny for your thoughts." She wanted to know why I was smiling. She seemed genuinely interested, and I told her, "I feel a burning in my heart that makes me smile." As I remembered that incident, I wondered if that heartfelt feeling might have been the Spirit speaking to me.

The next time the missionaries came, I told them this story. They explained that one of the ways the Spirit manifests Himself is by creating a burning in our hearts. They referenced a verse in the Book of Mormon: "And it came to pass that while they were thus conversing one with another, they heard a voice as if it came out of heaven; and (it) did cause their hearts to burn" (3 Nephi 11:3). This explanation allowed me to see that it was the Spirit that had warmed my heart.

I also told the missionaries that a year earlier I had cried through every hymn, prayer, and lesson during the Kingston Ward meetings. They told me that this was also a manifestation of the Spirit and shared another Book of Mormon verse: "And their hearts were swollen with joy, unto the gushing out of many tears" (3 Nephi 4:33). Similarly, my heart had been filled with love, and my tears had flowed. I began to realize there was a lot to understand about feeling the Spirit. Recognizing the Spirit allowed me to see ways that God had been attempting to communicate with me I had not seen.

CHAPTER 25

THE BOOK OF MORMON: A PERSONALIZED MESSAGE OF LOVE

OUR DISCUSSIONS WITH the missionaries centered on the Book of Mormon. When I went to the Unification Theological Seminary as a student in 1979, I bought a copy of the Book of Mormon and I had read a few passages occasionally ever since. The missionaries gave us a Book of Mormon reading assignment every time they came, and my casual approach to reading it changed to daily study. Alice and I read the assigned verses together every morning, and I read other passages on my own.

In the past, I had read the Book of Mormon as an observer of someone else's religion. It was true for them, but not for me. Reading the Book of Mormon with an awareness of the Spirit brought it to life. A few days after the missionaries' first visit, I was sitting on the couch reading the Book of Mormon, and it was entirely different. It was the same book I had had on my shelf for years. It was the same book I had read as a student in college. And yet it was not the same. I was no longer reading a book about someone else's religion. I was reading a book of divinely revealed truth intended for me. What had been a book of spiritual insight became an outpouring of God's love and guidance.

I had heard about exercising a particle of faith, and now I was doing it. I had sufficient belief to experiment with the truthfulness of the Book of Mormon. As I did, the Spirit opened the book to me; my heart stirred, and I felt hope. My hope wasn't just wishful thinking. It was hope in Jesus Christ, born of the Spirit's witness to Him as I read the Book of Mormon. My faith and hope blossomed as I read.

Once I discovered it was true for me, I started reading it in earnest. It fed me spiritually like nothing I had ever read before. I found more spiritual nourishment in reading even just one page than I had found in reading ten pages of anything else.

In addition to nourishing me spiritually, it gave me a way to find meaning in both the Bible and the Book of Mormon. The Book of Mormon prophet Nephi said, "I did liken all scriptures unto us" (1 Nephi 19:23). I began reading God's words aware that He had inspired the writing of the Bible and the Book of Mormon with me in mind. When I read familiar passages in the Old and New Testaments, I discovered love I had not felt before. The opening words of Handel's *Messiah* came to me: "Comfort ye, comfort ye my people" (Isaiah 40:1). For the first time, reading the scriptures was deeply comforting.

To reconnect with what it was like for me to be in my Book of Mormon class, I purchased the textbook for the course, *A Doctrinal Approach to the Book of Mormon.*[1] I prayerfully studied it. As I read and pondered the content, it was as if Brother Pearson was right there with me. I wondered why I hadn't recognized the Spirit when I was in his classes. Then I remembered how firmly I had held to my belief that everything there was to know about the Spirit was defined by my understanding of the Om vibration. I didn't come to know the Spirit because I was blinded by my existing beliefs.

Notes:

1. Pearson, G., & Bankhead, R. (1962). *A Doctrinal Approach to the Book of Mormon.* Salt Lake City, Utah: Bookcraft.

CHAPTER 26

PRAYING WITH REAL INTENT

FROM THE FIRST time the missionaries met with us, I was intentionally open and honest with them. Elder Stokes and Elder Bundy had something I wanted. Since my time as a student at BYU, missionaries for the Church of Jesus Christ of Latter-day Saints had stood out as spiritually alive. I saw studying with those two missionaries as a way to discover the secret to their aliveness.

In the past, I had unsuccessfully tried to be as alive as the missionaries I had met. Having tried and failed, I thought their spiritual vitality was the result of being born and raised in the Church by faithful parents. As we got to know the elders who taught us, they introduced us to other missionaries. It became evident that the joyful, vitality those various missionaries expressed was not the result of their lineage or upbringing. They were alive in Christ through their faith in Him and their obedience to His commandments. My viewpoint changed, and I could see that their aliveness was available to Alice and me.

Two weeks into our lessons, I became anxious. I was a leader in the Unification Church. What if these missionaries saw me as a big fish they were out to catch? My anxiety clouded my thoughts, and I shared my concern with Elder Stokes. I said, "I feel like I am being set up as a poster child of a convert to your church." He heard what I had to say and took me seriously. His way of listening showed me he was genuinely interested in me and my relationship with God. He wasn't just trying to get another baptism. His authentic concern dispelled my fear, and I was ready to move forward with our discussions.

The dedication of the missionaries moved me. They had left their homes far away, dressed in suits and ties and agreed to follow strict mission rules to have the privilege of teaching the gospel and bearing witness to Jesus Christ. The least I could do was express my respect by sincerely considering their message.

I had strongly held beliefs on every topic they addressed. I chose to listen to what they had to say without passing judgment on it. For example, they taught us about the Fall of Adam and Eve. In my mind, the Fall constituted a breakdown in God's plan. The missionaries provided a different interpretation. They bore witness that the Fall was necessary for the fulfillment of God's plan of salvation. In the past, I would have tried to reconcile those two perspectives or I would have rejected what they said in favor of what I already knew. Instead, I pondered what they had to say about the Fall.

During their visits, they always gave us an opportunity to ask questions. Once I asked, "What is the difference between immortality and eternal life?" I was trying to understand the declaration, "For behold, this is my work and my glory—to bring to pass the immortality and eternal life of man" (Moses 1:39, Pearl of Great Price). It seemed to me that those two words meant the same thing.

Elder Stokes explained, "Immortality is a free gift to all people through the atoning sacrifice of Jesus Christ. Every person who has ever lived on the earth will eventually regain a physical body and live forever. In contrast, eternal life is the opportunity to live forever in glory with Heavenly Father and Jesus Christ with our families." The Spirit intimated to me that this depiction of eternal life was Heavenly Father's vision for my family and me.

After every visit, Alice and I stayed up late talking about what the missionaries had taught us. Never in our marriage had we had such soul-searching conversations about religion. We were both considering what they had to say.

At one of our meetings, Elder Stokes asked me, "Do you believe Joseph Smith was a prophet?"

I said, "I do, and I believe that Moses, Mohammed, and Buddha were also prophets." I added, "The question you need to ask me is, 'Do you believe that Joseph Smith is a prophet who has a message for you?'"

Elder Stokes came right back at me. "Do you?"

I said, "No, I don't believe Joseph Smith is a prophet who has a message for me." Within the next few weeks and without giving it much thought, the Spirit quietly confirmed that Joseph Smith was a prophet who did have a message for me.

On another visit, they brought their mission president and his wife with them. This couple touched my heart with their embracing attitude. When I told the mission president we were members of the Unification Church, he acknowledged the Unification Church for promoting the value of marriage and the harmony between religions. His appreciation for the contributions of my church gave me a new idea of what it meant to be a Latter-day Saint. I had thought there was no place in the Church of Jesus Christ of Latter-day Saints for me with my vision of a brotherhood of people of all faiths.

I frequently heard members declare, "This is the one true church." It seemed like that statement invalidated other religions. Based on this mission president's endorsement of the Unification Church, I could see that the often-repeated "one true church" was a valid statement of faith that did not invalidate other churches. This change in perspective put to rest my concern that the Church was exclusive. The mission president's comment showed me it was possible to value the contributions of other religions and still be a respected Latter-day Saint.

Elder Stokes challenged me to set a baptismal date. I declined, but his challenge reminded me of the time I had prayed to know if the gospel was true as a student at BYU. It was time to ask again.

Because I had learned to get an answer I could trust by setting conditions, I created one. The condition consisted of three days of fasting and twenty-one days of prayer, with the purpose of answering the question, "Heavenly Father, how do You want me to understand the life and mission of Jesus Christ and my relationship to Him?" Once a week for three weeks, I fasted for twenty-four hours without food or water, and at least once a day for those three weeks I petitioned Heavenly Father for an answer to that question.

In the course of the condition, I reflected on the leaders of the Church whom I had either known personally or by reputation. By invoking their memory, I intended to attune myself with them to prepare for the answer to my prayer. I thought of my friend, Mitch Hunt, and Bette Hunt's father. My thoughts turned to all the presidents of the Church and many apostles. All the people who came to mind had won my respect through their testimonies or their way of being.

At a Kingston Ward meeting on the first Sunday in January 2000, a priest prayed over the bread representing the body of Christ and declared that eating the bread was an expression of willingness to keep the Lord's commandments. Those words touched me deeply. To capture the power of the moment, I started memorizing that prayer.

The next day, I completed my third day of fasting and my twenty-one days of prayer, but no answer came. I didn't have to wait long. The following morning my wife and I sat together for our daily study of the Book of Mormon. After a brief prayer, I read aloud chapter 9, verse 27 of 2 Nephi: "But wo unto him that has the law given, yea, that has all the commandments of God—." I stopped. The Spirit had prepared me for that moment by impressing on me the importance of keeping the commandments, and I knew the Lord was inviting me to obey His commandment to be baptized.

I started again at the beginning of the verse. "But wo unto him that has the law given, yea, that has all the commandments of God, like unto us, and that transgresseth them, and that wasteth the days of his probation, for awful is his state!"

From my training with Yogananda and Reverend Moon, I had a strong sense of the importance of preparing in this life for the world to come. The phrase "wasteth the days of his probation" carried a punch. Through the whispering of the Spirit, God himself was telling me, "You are squandering your time on earth! You need to be baptized!"

I continued reading: "O that cunning plan of the evil one! O the vainness, and the frailties, and the foolishness of men! When they are learned they think they are wise, and they hearken not unto the counsel of God, for they set it aside, supposing they know of themselves, wherefore, their wisdom is foolishness and it profiteth them not" (2 Nephi 9:28). Years earlier when I had prayed to know if the gospel was true, I had rejected the opportunity to know. This passage revealed that I had set aside the counsel of God. My behavior demonstrated that I thought I knew better than God the course I should follow in my life.

The answer to my prayer was clear, unmistakable, and compelling. I had known that if I prayed in faith, I would get a response confirming the truthfulness of the gospel. When I did, the Lord gave me a mandate to be baptized through the words of the Book of Mormon. Brother Pearson taught, "The Book of Mormon is the key to conversion." My conversion was a fulfillment of his declaration.

CHAPTER 27

BAPTISM, A NEW BEGINNING!

THE NEXT TIME I saw Elder Stokes, I told him, "I am getting baptized."

He said, "You don't seem happy about it."

"No, I am not," I said frankly.

"Why aren't you happy?" he asked.

"I am sorrowing that I didn't accept the gospel sooner," I said with regret.

He replied, "Take it to the Lord and let it go."

I did and found the joy I was missing.

About a week, I met with the Korean regional leader of the Unification Church to have a conversation about my choice to join the Church of Jesus Christ of Latter-day Saints. I thought he would ask me to reconsider, but he didn't. He said, "If that's what you think is best for you and your family, go right ahead." His response allowed me to let go of my heartfelt attachments to the Unification Church. Confident that becoming a Latter-day Saint would benefit both my family and me, I prepared to be baptized.

Surprisingly, my plans to join the Church created no controversy in the seminary community. The faculty and students accepted my decision as a personal choice. Some of my friends wanted to know if I had prayerfully considered what I was doing, but that was all.

Sean, a seminary faculty member, had a local radio program, and on the show, he interviewed people from different faith communities. As a prospective Latter-day Saint, he invited me to be a guest. To prepare myself for the interview, I pulled a copy of the Book of Mormon off the shelf in the seminary library. I opened it and started reading. The first words I read were, "Look not forward any more for another Messiah" (2 Nephi 25:16). I read on. "They need not look forward any more for a Messiah to come, for there should not any come, save it should be a false Messiah which should deceive the people; for there is save one Messiah spoken of by the prophets, and that Messiah is he who should be rejected of the Jews" (2 Nephi 25:18).

For years, I had thought of Reverend Moon as a messianic figure. As I read those passages under the influence of the Spirit, I gave up my view that Reverend Moon was fulfilling the prophecy of Christ's return. Fortified with a peaceful assurance that it was the Lord's will for me to accept the gospel, I went to the radio station for the interview. On the broadcast, I publicly declared my faith in Jesus Christ, further strengthening my resolve to be baptized.

I asked Bishop Avenius for his advice. He told me, "Don't look back!" I interpreted his guidance to mean I needed to focus on my new faith commitment. I looked for ways to be fully engaged. I bore my testimony at church, I invited my friends to hear the gospel, and I continued to study with the missionaries.

One day in January, Elder Stokes asked me to attend a special priesthood meeting. The same day as the meeting, I had a commitment to work as a librarian at the University of Bridgeport. The Spirit prompted me to keep the Sabbath day holy and to go to the priesthood meeting. After reflecting on this divine guidance, I called the university library, told them I would not be coming and went with Elder Stokes to the meeting.

Alice chose to join the Church on her own. Several times, a Brazilian member came to our home to teach her. Alice remarked, "It's magical there is someone who can teach me in Portuguese." She had questions about the gospel, and he patiently answered them. Alice asked, "What can you tell me about the mission of Adam?"

He told her, "The best way to find out about the mission of Adam is to go to the temple and, under the influence of the Spirit, learn about Adam's role in God's plan." She accepted his counsel and looked forward to learning more in the temple.

As she prayed about joining the Church, she received a witness that Jesus Christ is the only begotten son of God, and He is the Messiah. With this answer to her prayer, she committed to baptism. From her childhood observance of her faith as a Catholic, Alice loved receiving communion. She looked forward to taking bread and water in remembrance of the Savior every week as a member of the Church.

Once I had committed to baptism, I wrote to my college girlfriend, Jeannette, and let her know I was joining the Church. We had not been in touch for decades, and I had to get her address from the BYU Alumni Association. She received the news with joy. She told me that for more than twenty years, the Lord had been waking her in the night and asking her to pray for me. She went on to say that a month earlier, about the time the missionaries started teaching us, the Lord had told her she did not need to pray for me anymore. Her faithfulness in praying for me touched my heart. Her testimony served as a witness that the Lord knew me, loved me and waited for me to accept His invitation to be baptized.

A few days before my baptism, I had an interview with the mission president in the Poughkeepsie Ward building. He was there to meet with the full-time missionaries serving in the Hudson Valley. Before I met with him, I shared with the missionaries my conversion story. Those faithful young men and women serving as the Lord's representatives listened attentively and acknowledged me for choosing to follow Jesus Christ.

My interview with the mission president was wonderful. I shared with him things I had done that weighed on my heart. He listened to me with compassion. He met my openness and honesty with support and sound counsel. After our meeting, my heart was at peace, and I was ready to start a new life as a Latter-day Saint.

Alice and I chose to be baptized on the same day to maintain our unity in faith. I invited everyone I could think of to come. Many of the people I asked were old friends from BYU who lived out West. Most of them declined the invitation and promised to be with us in the temple when we consecrated our marriage as eternal the following year.

We scheduled our baptismal service to take place after church on Sunday, February 20, 2000. Most of the ward members were there, and several of my friends from the seminary came. Our special guests were my college roommate, Michael, and his wife, Tara. They had come from Fallon, Nevada. For Michael, my baptism was an answer to prayer. He told me that he and our other roommates had fasted and prayed for me to accept the gospel while we were at school together.

To begin the meeting, Carl led the congregation in "I Believe in Christ."[1] I chose that song to celebrate Jesus Christ as my lord and savior. After the opening prayer and a talk on baptism, everyone reassembled in the cultural hall to witness our baptism. At one end of the hall, two doors were open, revealing the baptismal font filled with water deep enough for us to be fully immersed. Elder Stokes baptized me, and Elder Bundy baptized Alice. When we had changed out of our white baptismal clothing, we rejoined our guests in the chapel.

The service resumed with the Brazilian member who taught Alice singing, "I Stand All Amazed."[2] I had asked him to sing that song because years earlier, as a student at BYU, its precious words moved me: "Oh, it is wonderful that He should care for me enough to die for me! Oh, it is wonderful, wonderful to me!" Following his song and a talk about the gift of the Holy Ghost, Michael confirmed me as a member of the Church and conferred upon me the gift of the Holy Ghost. I felt the authority and power of the ceremony. Bishop Avenius then confirmed Alice as a member of the Church and bestowed upon her the gift of the Holy Ghost. Michael told me later that he had been conscious of the Spirit speaking through him as he pronounced a blessing upon me on behalf of God.

To conclude, we sang, "The Spirit of God."[3] This was the hymn sung at the dedication of the Kirtland Temple, the first temple of the Church. I chose it to invoke the Lord's vision for temple work. My heart was set on going to the temple. I put so much attention on going to the temple that I minimized the value of my baptismal covenant. In making that covenant, I promised the Lord I would bear witness to Him, keep His commandments, and lift others' burdens. For His part, the Lord promised to guide me and nourish me spiritually. This was an important covenant, and I was acting like it was just a prerequisite to going to the temple.

I gained a deeper appreciation for the significance of my baptism a few years later. On the Saturday following President Hinckley's death at the beginning of 2008, his successor, President Thomas S. Monson, addressed a worldwide leadership conference. As he spoke, I had the distinct impression he was the Lord's chosen prophet. The Spirit prompted me to write to him and bear my testimony that he was a prophet and chosen by the Lord to lead the Church. I hesitated. I didn't want to bother him with my personal revelation. Two days later, Alice and I were in the temple, and again I had an impression I should write to President Monson. After that second prompting, I wrote to him.

A few weeks later, I received a reply. President Monson acknowledged my support and thanked me for it. Then I noticed the date on the letter—February 20, 2008. It was the anniversary of our baptism. Through that letter, the Spirit let me know that the Lord remembered the day I made my covenant with Him. Baptism is a much more sacred covenant than I had realized. I may forget, but the Lord will never forget the day I made my first covenant with Him.

Notes:

1. McConkie, B. (1972). "I Believe in Christ." In *Hymns of The Church of Jesus Christ of Latter-day Saints*, 1985. Salt Lake City, Utah: The Church of Jesus Christ of Latter-day Saints.

2. Gabriel, C. (1898). "I Stand All Amazed." In *Hymns of The Church of Jesus Christ of Latter-day Saints*, 1985. Salt Lake City, Utah: The Church of Jesus Christ of Latter-day Saints.

3. Phelps, W. (1836). "The Spirit of God." In *Hymns of The Church of Jesus Christ of Latter-day Saints*, 1985. Salt Lake City, Utah: The Church of Jesus Christ of Latter-day Saints.

Chapter 28

Life as a Latter-day Saint

As a member of the Church, commandments I had always kept had a different effect. This was particularly true with paying tithes. I learned about tithing in the Methodist Church membership classes I took when I was fourteen. Ever since then, I had faithfully paid a tithe of 10 percent of my income to whatever church I belonged to. However, I had never noticed the fulfillment of the Lord's promise to open the windows of heaven and pour out blessings upon me as promised in the scriptures (Malachi 3:10). Once I started paying my tithe to the Church of Jesus Christ of Latter-day Saints, the Lord began pouring out blessings on me. They were never quantifiable or predictable, yet I knew I was blessed for keeping this commandment.

When I joined the Church, I put my family first. This was a big change. My priority had always been my work and ministry. I began spending more time with Alice, David, and Patricia. It is a tradition of the Church to have a weekly Family Home Evening. It is a time for spiritual teaching, prayer, and activities at home with your family. Alice and I adopted this practice of meeting together each week as a family. The favorite part for David and Patricia was the games we played.

Before my baptism, Bishop Avenius told me, "We need you." I didn't take him seriously. As a member, I could see that there was a need for people who were willing to serve. In less than a month, I accepted a calling. A calling is a request from God coming from one of His designated representatives to provide service in some way. My first calling was to be the

Sunday School president. The best thing about being the Sunday School president was that I got to attend the ward council meetings. I loved fellowshipping with the other ward leaders and counseling with them, under the influence of the Spirit, about how to lift up and care for ward members.

On the day of my baptism, Bishop Avenius ordained me as a priest. Soon I began participating in the defining ceremony of our weekly sacrament meetings. During that meeting, two priests partner in blessing the emblems of the body and blood of Jesus Christ. One blesses the bread, and the other blesses the water. Each week, I knelt at the sacrament table and offered one of the prayers. During those prayers, I knew that I was acting on behalf of God and creating a sacred moment of worship.

Elder Stokes encouraged us to go to the temple to perform baptisms for our kindred dead as soon as possible. In March, I went on a trip with the youth of our ward to the Washington D.C. Temple. I rode down with Brian Wootan. Brother Wootan had come to our home with two missionaries several years earlier to deliver a Church video we requested in response to a public service announcement we had seen on television. When he visited us, he left me with a good impression, and I wanted to get to know him better. The long drive to Washington, D.C. gave me that opportunity.

Like me, he had gone to BYU, and he told me he had been on the rugby team. I asked him, "Do you know John Seggar, the rugby coach?" Dr. Seggar had come to the seminary for a theological dialog when I was a seminary student. Brother Wootan said, "Yes, he was my coach." He then shared with me what he was like as a coach. Dr. Seggar had made a lasting impact on both of our lives, and now the Lord had drawn Brother Wootan and me together. Our shared connection to Dr. Seggar became a foundation for the friendship that grew between us.

Bishop Avenius impressed my friend Sean when they met at our baptism, and Sean invited him to speak in a ministry class at the Seminary. Bishop Avenius was the director of a

New York State agency, and he was a successful business owner. He accepted the invitation to speak and talked about integrating your faith into every aspect of your life. He embodied the principle he taught. His example of living an integrated life inspired me to try to do the same.

To encourage me to receive my patriarchal blessing, Elder Stokes shared with me that his patriarchal blessing was a source of strength and comfort to him. His testimony moved me, and I made a request to receive my own. Alice was also eager to receive counsel from Heavenly Father for her life through a patriarchal blessing. In May 2000, the local patriarch bestowed on Alice and me this once-in-a-lifetime personal revelation from God. As the patriarch laid his hands on my head, I knew Heavenly Father loved me. The patriarch's wife recorded the blessing, and a few weeks later, the transcript came in the mail. Whenever I read it, the Spirit ministers to me through its sacred words.

Encouraged by my conversion, Elder Stokes saw the students at the Seminary as prepared to receive the gospel. With the intent of building relationships of trust with them, he organized a soccer match between the missionaries serving in the Hudson Valley and the seminary students. It thrilled me to see the brotherhood between them as they played together. As a result of his efforts, Elder Stokes and his companion had several teaching opportunities with seminarians.

Late in May 2000, the mission president transferred Elder Stokes to another ward. I depended on Elder Stokes to bolster my faith, and I was afraid I would not feel the Spirit as powerfully when he departed. I had no need for concern. The Lord was watching over me.

The day after Elder Stokes left, a new family moved into the ward, and I helped them unload their belongings from a truck. In the process, I found a new friend, David. His friendship filled my need for a close friend in the gospel. He had moved to Kingston to complete a residency in podiatry, and he was a warm-hearted person.

David's friendship was an expression of God's love for me. Sometimes he called just to see how I was doing. He wasn't my home teacher, and he didn't have any reason to call. David just wanted to say hello and connect. Not only did I bond with David, but Alice also found a close friend in his wife, Fatima, who was from Brazil. They loved to be together. Effortlessly, their friendship deepened over time.

Once I joined the Church, I started looking for employment opportunities outside the Unification Movement. The Unification Theological Seminary was an interfaith seminary, and it would have been consistent with the seminary's mission to have a member of the Church on the faculty; nevertheless, I wanted to move on. I didn't want to train seminary students to be leaders for the Unification Church while I was in a period of faith formation. I gave notice I would be leaving at the end of August 2000.

As I looked for work, I discovered that the best paying job for me was as a library media specialist in a public school. I contacted the School of Library and Information Science at Rutgers University where I received my library degree and enrolled in a program to become certified as a school librarian. My certification was still pending when I applied for jobs. The school districts where I interviewed chose other applicants because I had not yet received my certification. My job search stalled, and my wife and I were nervous.

I called Elder Stokes for his advice, and he asked me, "Have you fasted about finding a job?"

I said, "No, I haven't."

In his question, I found the answer I sought. Alice and I both fasted and prayed for guidance. In response, I found peace. I was worry-free and confident I would have a new job when the time came. The answer to Alice's fast was more specific. The Spirit told her that when I completed my work at the Seminary, I would have another job.

My new position came just as the Spirit promised Alice. On my final day as the seminary librarian, the faculty and staff held a farewell luncheon for me. From there, I went directly to an interview at Storm King School, a private, coeducational high school. At the end of our meeting, they offered to hire me as their librarian, and I accepted. This was the answer to our prayers.

In July, after an interview with the bishop, he determined I was ready to be ordained as an elder. At my request, Elder Stokes came and performed the ordination. As he placed his hands on my head, I received a confirming witness of the sacredness of the priesthood he conferred upon me. As an elder, I had the priesthood authority to invoke blessings like the one I received from Carl when I was a student at the Seminary.

The following Sunday for the first time, I served in my capacity as an elder. The Elders Quorum President brought some olive oil to the Elders Quorum meeting and invited me to consecrate the oil for the healing of the sick. With the authority to act on behalf of God I had as an elder, I consecrated the oil. What a powerful experience! When I finished, I knew I had been an instrument in the hands of the Lord. I have exercised my authority as an elder hundreds of times since then to give blessings of healing and comfort. Nevertheless, the simple ceremony of dedicating that oil for God's purposes stands out in my memory and continues to remind me of the sacred privilege it is to be His representative.

Elder Stokes was from Nampa, Idaho, and Nampa was the home of my childhood friend, Miriam. Her brother, David, had awakened my interest in the Church when I was in junior college, and her mother, Emma, had suggested I go to BYU. I showed Elder Stokes a Christmas card from Miriam with a photograph of her family. Elder Stokes thought he recognized one of her daughters, but he wasn't sure. Not long after that, I had a chance to talk with Elder Stokes' mother on the phone, and I asked her if she knew Miriam. She said they were in the same ward and she knew her well. As she spoke, the Spirit bore witness to me that Elder Stokes had been sent to find me in response to Miriam's prayers.

In November 2000, I took my wife and children to visit my family in California. My brother Bert was the only one who made a comment about Alice and me joining the Church. He said, "It's a big commitment to join the Church of Jesus Christ of Latter-day Saints." He knew some Latter-day Saints, and he had seen how much time they invested in their church activities. I knew what he meant. It was a big commitment, and I liked big commitments.

Our trip to California coincided with Elder Stokes' return from his mission. On returning home, he transitioned from Elder Stokes, full-time missionary, to Kalab Stokes, returned missionary. We went back to New York by way of Nampa, to visit Miriam and to attend Kalab's homecoming. We arrived the day after Thanksgiving. To my surprise, Miriam's mother and her brother, David, were visiting from Utah. They were there to attend the Eagle Court of Honor for Miriam's son that night. It was actually a double Court of Honor for Miriam's son and Kalab's brother. What a joy to see Emma and David and find out I would be able to attend the Court of Honor! The alignment of timing and people amazed me. This was more than a coincidence. It was a divinely staged event. At the Court of Honor, Kalab and I, both of us Eagle Scouts, sat together as those two young men received their Eagle awards.

We stayed at Miriam's home, and her whole family embraced us. Emma and David were staying there too. What a reunion! We shared precious memories and testimonies. While spending time with Miriam, David, and Emma, the Lord impressed on my heart that He had sent this family to Oroville, California in the 1950s to prepare the way for me to accept the gospel. Being with them strengthened my faith.

The next morning, Alice and I went to the Boise Temple with Kalab. When he introduced us at the front desk as recent converts, one of the men greeted me warmly and said, "It is true." His simple statement has returned to me frequently over the years as a reminder that the gospel is true. In the temple, Kalab baptized Alice and me for some of my ancestors.

We thrilled in the outpouring of the Spirit affirming the value of that work for my kindred dead.

One of the most meaningful parts of our visit to Nampa was Kalab's homecoming. In the sacrament meeting of his home ward, he talked about his mission. He then introduced me, and I shared my testimony. Emma Goddard was sitting in the front row, and I publicly acknowledged her for the difference she had made in my life by suggesting I go to BYU.

Back in New York in December 2000, one year after we first met with the missionaries who taught us, I declared in a church meeting, "My experience of being a member of the Church of Jesus Christ of Latter-day Saints is this: it only gets better." Through the course of that year, no matter what challenges arose, the Spirit was right there, ready to support me in dealing with them. To this day, my testimony remains the same: It only gets better.

CHAPTER 29

"WHAT TOOK YOU SO LONG?"

IN JANUARY 2001, almost a year after Alice and I had become members of the Church, I received a phone call from President Ricks, our stake president. In his position as stake president, he presided over nine congregations of the Church of Jesus Christ of Latter-day Saints in the Hudson Valley. He had called to ask me to address the evening session of the upcoming stake conference regarding my conversion. I gladly accepted. As I hung up the phone, the Spirit impressed on me that his invitation was a request from the Lord. With a sense of divine purpose, I prepared my talk. I intended to provide an empowering testimony and to invite the Spirit to confirm my words.

During the opening hymn, I sat in front of the congregation at the Newburgh, New York Stake Center waiting for my turn to speak. Sitting beside me was Elder M. Russell Ballard of the Quorum of the Twelve Apostles, who had come to release President Ricks and identify the new stake president. My time came, and I gave my talk. When I sat down, Elder Ballard stood to speak. Standing at the podium, he turned to me and asked, "Brother Bowers, what took you so long?" He didn't expect an answer, but he started me thinking—what did take me so long?

As I pondered Elder Ballard's question, I realized I could have taken an interest in the Church in high school. I had a strong Christian upbringing. My grandmother and my mother instilled in me a love for the scriptures, and I had a foundation of faith in Christ as a Methodist. I even had several friends who were Latter-day Saints, and I had been looking for a more fulfilling life of faith. Yet it had never entered my mind as a teenager to consider what the Church had to offer.

When I identified Latter-day Saints as good people, I became curious about what made them different. To satisfy my curiosity, I met with missionaries from the Church. While I was meeting with them, I was preparing a song from Handel's *Messiah* for a singing competition. The words of the song penetrated my heart, and I knew the Lord would come again. I see now that the Spirit provided me with that witness to Christ in answer to the prayers of the missionaries. I realize that at that time the Spirit had extended to me an invitation to accept Jesus Christ as my savior.

Yogananda's teachings served as my frame of reference while I was at BYU. I rejected anything inconsistent with his message. For example, he advocated for being reverent in preparation for public worship. When I went to church meetings at BYU, I came in, sat down, and prayerfully waited for the service to begin. At the same time, I was silently judgmental of the socializing going on around me. After my baptism, I read a biography of President David O. McKay, who was president of the Church when I arrived at BYU. I discovered he had made an ongoing effort to encourage reverence in church meetings. His patient, loving approach to advocating for reverence moved me. I gave up my critical attitude and made a personal commitment to invite the presence of the Spirit in church meetings.

Yogananda's guidance also informed my attitude toward the testimonies that members shared. He taught that the presence of God is intended to impact our lives right now, in the moment. As I listened to people share, I assessed whether their testimonies were authentic expressions of the current reality of God's presence in their lives. I dismissed any comments that did not meet my expectations. As a member, I have learned that the Lord loves everything people have to share as an expression of their faith. Now I listen on behalf of God, and I find value in whatever people say.

Yogananda said churches are often little more than theological social clubs. I assessed the relationships among members to see if the Church was a theological social club, and I concluded that it was. After joining the Church, I discovered that socializing provides the Spirit with an opportunity to minister to us in ways we don't always recognize. As we fellowship with each other, the Lord builds his church and refines our character.

Yogananda also had an inclusive view of the various faith traditions in the world. From his perspective, I thought of the Church of Jesus Christ of Latter-day Saints as part of the brotherhood of all religions. Joseph Smith asserted that abiding by the precepts of the Book of Mormon draws people near to God.[1] I understood these precepts to be universal principles. The Book of Mormon teaches the importance of service, prayer, study, obedience, and worship which are fundamental to most religions. Surrounded by people who focused on the uniqueness of the Church, I put my attention on what it had in common with other belief systems.

While I was at BYU, I also fell into the trap of using reason to try to understand things that are discerned by faith. For example, I heard a statement made by Lorenzo Snow, a former Church president, "As man now is, God once was; as God is, man may become."[2] I see now that this is an expression of God's love and His vision of our divine potential. At the time, it didn't seem reasonable to have God be a man first. I reasoned that during the time God was mortal there would be no God. By trusting in my assessment, I justified clinging to my existing beliefs.

When Brother Pearson taught that following Jesus Christ with a broken heart gives us inner peace and freedom. I missed the point. The blessings that come from a broken heart depend upon faith in Jesus Christ. Through faith in Him, I can now claim the blessings of peace and freedom.

As Brother Pearson explained the ways of knowing, he was inviting me to discover revelation as a natural part of daily life rather than the result of meditation and prayer over an extended period. I resisted his invitation to discover a new way of knowing. Just as Brother Pearson taught, revelation has become both accessible and reliable.

Two things expedited my journey. First, I announced in the BYU alumni magazine that I had received my PhD and I was the library director at the Unification Theological Seminary. Without knowing it, my announcement invoked the prayers of readers. No one has specifically told me they prayed for me; however, the Spirit has let me know that many people offered prayers on my behalf as a result of my bulletin.

The other thing that expedited my journey was having Elder Yuba and his companion to dinner at the beginning of 1999. Their visit served as an invitation to the Spirit to touch our hearts. I was following President Rasband's counsel on how to share the gospel. I adapted his guidance to fulfill my purpose; however, the Spirit fulfilled President Rasband's intent. Our dinner meeting left both Alice and me impressed with what was available to us in the Church of Jesus Christ of Latter-day Saints.

From my exposure to the Church, I had informed opinions about many of the aspects of it. I was confident the Church constituted the restoration of first century Christianity. I was convinced there was great value in the redeeming work done in the temples of the Church, and I had personally witnessed the capacity of the leaders of the Church to act on behalf of God.

These insights made no difference for me until I became aware of the Spirit. At that point, what I already knew became personally empowering. From the time Elder Stokes distinguished the Spirit for me, it did not take long for me to accept the gospel. I went from being an observer of someone else's religion to being a committed member in a matter of weeks. Once I discerned the Spirit, I rapidly progressed toward baptism.

Notes:

1. Smith, Joseph. (1981). "Introduction." *Book of Mormon*. Salt Lake City, Utah: The Church of Jesus Christ of Latter-day Saints.
2. Snow, E. (1984). *Biography and Family Record of Lorenzo Snow*. Salt Lake City, Utah: Deseret News, 46.

CHAPTER 30

SEALED IN THE JORDAN RIVER TEMPLE

IN DECEMBER 2000, I called Rebecca Hunt Monson and said, "Rebecca, Alice and I are going to make our temple covenants in the Jordan River Temple on March 17. Will you join us?"

There was silence on the line. She broke the silence with, "Are you sure?" She had seen other people make plans to go to the temple and when the time came, they didn't go. I replied, "Yes, I am sure! We will be there on March 17." Hearing my conviction, she accepted our invitation to be with us in the temple.

For me, going to the temple was a big deal. I had vivid memories of the uplifting impact of temple service on the lives of my friends at BYU. At my baptism, my heart was set on Alice and I making our temple covenants. As new members of the Church, we waited a year before we did so. Our priority was to covenant with the Lord to be an eternal family. We would make this covenant in a temple ceremony called a sealing, in which the Lord promises to preserve and sustain our marriage and family on earth and in heaven. Our part of the covenant would be to keep His commandments.

Our plan was coming together, and we would soon be fully benefiting from the blessings of the temple. We chose to go to a temple in Utah for the convenience of people we knew out West. As our temple date approached, I started asking people to join us. On the top of my list was Donna Bowers Harding and her husband, Terry. They accepted our invitation and invited us to go with them on a tour of Temple Square the day before the big event. When we met with them, Donna and I acknowledged the fulfillment of the Lord's plan for me to join the Church.

It was important to me for the Hunt family to come. They had served as a powerful example of gospel living. Their family relationships defined for me what it meant to be a Latter-day Saint. I saw them as saints in every sense of the word. In addition to Rebecca, David and Bette also accepted our invitation.

The Hunts announced they were going to put on a reception following our sealing. Bette's sister served in the Jordan River Temple, and she lived in a condominium complex right behind it. She arranged for us to use the common room for our reception. The Hunts took total responsibility for providing a cake and refreshments. Their enthusiastic response to our invitation brought magic to the event.

Alice and I had visited Arlene, my scoutmaster's wife, on a trip to California in 1993. Her husband had died, and she now lived in Oregon. She accepted our invitation and came with one of her sons, who had been in Boy Scouts with me. To have Arlene and her son with us in the temple affirmed the Lord had been watching over me during my formative years.

In 1979, I met a Church Education Director while I was attending the Poughkeepsie Ward. He had invited me to have lunch with his family, and I had fond memories of spending time in his home. I wanted to ask him, but I didn't even remember his name. My wife and I were sitting in the Poughkeepsie Ward building in February 2001, waiting to meet with the stake president. Other people were waiting for interviews as well, and I mentioned having met the Church Education Director who served in the area in 1979. One of the sisters waiting with us overheard me and said, "You mean Bert Hoffman." She told me he was living in Utah. I invited him to join us in the temple, and he gladly accepted.

Just after I became a seminary student in 1979, I met Elder Meservy, who was serving his mission in New York. His father had been my Old Testament professor at BYU. I wondered if

Brother Meservy would have any recollection of me. I took a chance and called him. It had been thirty years since I took a class with him, but he still remembered me. I told him my story of meeting his son when he was serving his mission, and I extended an invitation to him to be with us in the temple. Brother Meservy came with his wife and son.

Martell and Marian Blair had known me all my life. They had been playing bridge with my parents the night I was born. Martell was raised as a Latter-day Saint. After his marriage to Marian, each Sunday he went to his church, and she went to hers. She saw that religion was keeping them apart and joined the Church of Jesus Christ of Latter-day Saints to unify their family. Mart and Marian came from California to join us in the Jordan River Temple. How precious it was for them to be there! They had been a loving presence in my life since day one.

Mart told his nephew, who was part of the staff at the Jordan River Temple, that we were coming. When I walked into the temple, he stepped right up and greeted me by name. It was as if I was being personally greeted by the Savior: "Welcome home!"

Glenn Pearson, my Book of Mormon professor, helped me form the foundation of my testimony of the gospel. As I prepared for my baptism, I tried to contact him. I found one of his sons, and he told me his father had died less than a year earlier. The Spirit reassured me he knew I was getting baptized. I speculated that when he died, the Lord asked him, "Where is Tom Bowers?" It seemed to me the Lord had personally given Brother Pearson an assignment to bring me to the Church, and he wasn't finished with his work on the earth until he did. Surely, even after his death, Brother Pearson played a role in the missionaries finding us. When it was time for us to go to the temple, I invited Brother Pearson's widow, and she came with one of her sons and his wife. Their presence provided closure to Brother Pearson's contribution to my conversion.

Albert Choules was the president of the New York City Mission for the Church in 1983 while I was a Unification Church leader. I had visited him in his apartment at the Lincoln Center, and he had given me a copy of *A Marvelous Work and a Wonder*. I thought it would be great if he could be with us in the temple. Looking through the book he gave me, I found his business card. With the outdated information on his card, I located him in Salt Lake City. He remembered having met me, accepted my invitation, and came to be with us.

Michael, my college roommate, and his wife, Tara, jumped at the chance to come. I asked Michael why he was eager to make the trip from Nevada. He said, "I want to complete the journey with you." He added, "Tara and I make a practice of supporting people we know when they go to the temple for the first time. It is always marvelous to be in the temple with people we know."

Michael was still in touch with Ed, one of our Alpha Phi Omega fraternity brothers. Michael invited him, and I had no idea he would be there. What a surprise! He came all the way from Iowa.

Jeannette, my college girlfriend, came from California with her husband, her sister and her husband, and her mother. What an outpouring of support and love! The Lord had prompted her to pray for me for more than twenty years. In the temple, she witnessed with her family the fulfillment of her prayers.

Duane and I were good friends in graduate school. I knew both Duane and his wife from our days together at BYU. They generously offered to let us stay in their home in West Valley City while we were in Utah. We renewed our friendship, and Duane supported us with his presence in the temple.

Several of the young men and women who had been missionaries at the time of our conversion also came, including Kalab Stokes, who helped me recognize the Spirit, and Takeshi Yuba, who taught Alice to pray to God and *for* her ancestors.

The event would not have been complete without Emma Goddard. She came with her daughter, Miriam, and one of her granddaughters.

The minute I entered the temple, it was as if I was in God's presence. What it was like for me to go to other temples for baptisms was just a hint of what I felt on that occasion. Just walking in the door gave me clarity and focus. Gone was my striving to connect to whomever I was as a person. I was at peace with myself. Gone was my way of anticipating what was going to happen next. Each moment was an experience unto itself. What a dramatic transition from the world outside to a realm of divine well-being!

Before we went for our sealing, we received instruction and made covenants to support us in our sojourn on earth and in the life to come. Before the instruction began, I looked around the room and saw row after row of my friends. What a joy to be in that sacred place and catch a glimpse of people I had not seen in years!

At one point in the meeting, the light became brighter to symbolize a greater manifestation of the Spirit. Coincident with the raising of the lights, I felt the Spirit more strongly. At the end of the meeting, one goes from the instruction room into the celestial room, which represents being in the presence of God. There in that holy place, I exchanged whispered greetings and warm embraces with my friends. In the background, I felt an empowering divine presence. The quiet was alive! The peace embraced us. The listening presence of God was unmistakable. An assurance that goodness and mercy would follow me all the days of my life and I would dwell in the house of the Lord forever filled my heart.

It was time for our sealing. With our friends looking on, we covenanted with the Lord to be a couple forever. Afterward, David and Patricia came in, and the officiator blessed us as a family to be together on earth and in heaven. Through these sealing ceremonies, I entered into a new relationship with the Lord. I was no longer just in a personal covenant with Him.

I was also in a covenant with Him as a husband and a father, expanding my accountability.

After our sealing, we walked around to the back of the temple for the reception. There, I introduced Alice to my friends who had known me at various times in my life. They all extended to us their heartfelt congratulations and best wishes. It was a once-in-a-lifetime event.

I had a passing idea that it was a wonderful social gathering. The Spirit interrupted my thought and impressed on my heart, "No, this is not a social gathering. The Lord has created this event so that you can be face-to-face with the people He has put in your path throughout your life." It was evident to me the Lord had selected each of them to prepare me to accept the gospel and had prompted them to pray for me. He wanted me to grasp the ongoing effort He had made to bring me home.

The impact of being in the Jordan River Temple had unprecedented staying power. For three weeks, I basked in joy and glory entirely new to me. A month later, Alice and I went to the Boston Temple to serve as proxies for our ancestors to make temple blessings available to them. In a different temple without the presence of our many friends, I felt the same vivid, palpable, loving presence of God. Our Utah temple experience proved to be a preview of what we could expect every time we went to a temple.

After we returned from Utah, I started looking for a position as a public school librarian. I found a posting and submitted my résumé. Before long, they called me in for an interview and offered me the job. It was an act of God. The man I replaced had decided to retire late in the school year, and the school district needed to find someone quickly. I was the only applicant who had the necessary qualifications. They had to hire me or reopen the search. In my new job, I was going to make more money, receive greater benefits, and have a shorter commute and better working hours. The Spirit revealed to me that the Lord gave me this opportunity on the foundation of our temple covenants.

As a result of drawing closer to the Lord in the temple, I had a deeper appreciation for how He had patiently waited for me to accept the gospel. Also, Alice and I had the peace of mind that we would be together with our children for eternity. As a bonus, I got a better job. Going to the temple was both profound and life-changing.

CHAPTER 31

CALLED TO SERVE

SISTER AVENIUS CAME to our home when we were new to the Church. As I greeted her, she saw the bent closer on our screen door. Before I could say anything, she was on her way to the hardware store to get a new one. Within minutes, she came back and installed it. Her spontaneous act of kindness moved me. She showed me that service is a way for the Spirit to touch people's hearts.

As a new member, my service was an expression of duty. As I accepted leadership responsibilities, the Lord taught me to serve as an expression of His love rather than as the fulfillment of an obligation. The Lord gave me ample opportunities to learn to serve in His way. Six months after making my temple covenants, I accepted a call to be a counselor to the bishop. As I performed my duties, the Lord worked through me to express His love.

While I was serving in the bishopric, I received an assignment to be the home teacher to Tim Burgess, a young man who had not been to church for a while. I was unable to locate him, and I asked a ward member to contact his father to get Tim's address. His father did not respond. For more than a year, I kept praying for Tim, hoping someday I would find him.

One Sunday, a young couple came to church, and I introduced myself. When I asked the young man his name, he said, "My name is Tim Burgess." What a joy to finally meet him! He had come to church with his girlfriend, who was visiting from Utah. I got his contact information and scheduled a home teaching visit. My companion and I drove to the run-down three-story house he shared with other college students. We climbed the narrow stairs to Tim's small attic room. We found a place to sit, and Tim sat on his bed. We gave our lesson, had a conversation, and prayed together. As we did, there was an unusually strong presence of the Spirit.

His girlfriend went back to Utah, and I thought Tim would stop coming to church. On the contrary, he became more active. Tim accepted a call as a Sunday School teacher and taught my son's class. David thought Tim was cool because he played the guitar and worked in a computer game store. Tim came to our home for dinner and joined us for our Family Home Evening. It was great to have him as part of our family activities.

In the summer of 2004, the bishop confided in me that he was going to ask to be released from the responsibility of his calling to care for his wife. She had been diagnosed with a serious illness and needed his full attention. I began to wonder who would receive the call to be the next bishop. Two weeks later, the stake president asked me to meet with him and to bring Alice. It was a shock to both of us when he asked me to be the bishop of the Kingston Ward. It was a big responsibility. I turned to the Lord for assurance that this was His will. He confirmed it was, and I accepted the calling.

It took more than a brief prayer for Alice to accept my calling as the bishop. She couldn't see herself in the role of a bishop's wife and thought they had made a mistake because we were so young in the Church.

She told the outgoing bishop's wife, "I don't feel adequate to meet the expectations of me while my husband serves as the bishop."

She told Alice, "Be who you are and don't worry." Alice took comfort in her words, and the Lord worked through her to provide loving support to the members of the ward and me.

I thought serving in the bishopric was good training for my new calling. I discovered that nothing could have fully prepared me. As I adapted to my new responsibilities, I benefited from the prayers of my counselors and the ward members. In spite of my limitations, the Lord used me to fulfill His purposes. I found myself speaking kind words in situations where kind words would not have ordinarily come to me. In answer to my prayers, the Spirit carried my counsel to people's hearts. I came to know what it's like to serve on behalf of the Lord as a bishop. Nevertheless, it was a challenging responsibility.

I found the courage to carry on from a Bible verse, "God is our refuge and strength, a very present help in trouble" (Psalms 46:1). The Lord filled the gap between my ability and what He needed to have done. However, I did not always rely on the Lord. When I did not depend on Him, I exhausted myself.

As bishop, my plan was for all the active adult members of our ward to enjoy the blessings of the temple. One of the first people I talked with about going to the temple was Tim Burgess. I interviewed him in preparation for his ordination as an elder and before he made his temple covenants. Within a year, his girlfriend, who was now his fiancée, returned to New York for their marriage. To celebrate the occasion, Tim's parents came. His father had been the bishop of the Kingston Ward in the mid-1990s, and many ward members greeted him warmly. When we met, he said, "You look familiar."

I said, "We might have met when you were living in Kingston."

He replied, "I think it was something else."

When his wife greeted me, she said, "I know you—you're Tom Bowers."

Surprised, I asked, "How do you know me?"

She said, "You were a member of the Alpha Phi Omega fraternity at BYU." She and her husband had been married at the time, and she had participated in some of the activities of our fraternity.

It dawned on me that I had been watching over my fraternity brother's son! With this realization of who Tim's father was, I went to him and said, "The reason I seem familiar is that we are fraternity brothers." We embraced, and my tears flowed.

Again, the Lord showed me He had been watching over me these many years. The Spirit assured me the Lord had sent Brother Burgess and his family to New York to find me and bring me to the Church. It was fitting that I had prayed to find Tim. The strong outpouring of the Spirit I had felt on my first home teaching visit with Tim now made sense. The Spirit was working to draw Tim closer to the Church and preparing me to receive a witness of the Lord's love.

In my efforts to inspire ward members to go to the temple, I met with a husband and wife, Billy and Mary. They accepted my challenge to prepare to make their temple covenants. After Billy made his temple covenants, we frequently went to the temple together. In the process, we became close friends.

Billy was a humble man without much schooling. He had spent his life doing simple manual labor. Billy was one of the kindest, most patient, loving people I have ever met. He loved to declare God's word and did so with authority. He always began by saying, "The Heavenly Father says," and continued with a statement of a gospel principle. He also had several colorful expressions. Regarding swearing, he said, "I wouldn't write those words on the bottom of my shoe, let alone put them in my mouth."

We loved to sing together at the local brain trauma center. I played the piano, and Billy stood beside the old upright as we sang many favorites such as "You Are My Sunshine,"[1] "Take Me Out to the Ball Game,"[2] and "God Bless America."[3] The residents joined in, and we all had a great time.

One day, I got word Billy had gone to the hospital for tests. He wasn't feeling well and thought he should find out what was bothering him. He was seventy years old and had always been active. It didn't occur to me his life might be in danger. When I arrived at the hospital, he was on his way to surgery. He was in good spirits and explained what the doctors were going to do. My arrival was providential. The few words we exchanged before he went to surgery were some of his last. Billy passed away after the operation without regaining consciousness. As I mourned his loss, I pondered the privilege it was to share Billy's walk with the Lord here on earth.

Not long after I became the bishop, a member with autism moved into the ward from New York City. Ken was a dental appliance technician by trade, and he was close to retirement. He moved to the area to be near his mother. Because of his autism, Ken said things that were socially awkward, and people were uncomfortable with how close he stood when he conversed with them. He dressed in shabby clothing and was careless with his grooming. Some of the members of the ward thought he was a threat to the children. I addressed their concerns and created a safe environment for the children by making sure Ken was never alone with any of them. At the same time, I made sure he felt welcome by providing him with the assurance that we loved him.

Shortly after Ken's arrival in Kingston, the Manhattan Temple president, John Stone, told me he knew Ken. Ken had been phoning him weekly for twenty years. President Stone said that in all those years, Ken had never been as happy as he was in the Kingston Ward. In response to President Stone's remarks, I renewed my commitment to embrace Ken.

After five years, Ken found out he had cancer. As a result, he wasn't able to come to church. I then learned he was in hospice care in Newburgh. On our way to a priesthood meeting, Carl and I visited him. I was glad to see Ken, though I could see he was dying.

A few days later, the Spirit prompted me to contact John Stone. I called the public affairs office where he had served after completing his tenure as temple president. The receptionist informed me that Brother Stone had moved to Utah, but he was in town for a few days visiting his daughter. The receptionist gave me his daughter's number, and I left a message for Brother Stone telling him Ken was in hospice care. Later that day, I received a call from Brother Stone's daughter. She said that when her parents received my voicemail, they contacted Ken's brother, found out where Ken was in hospice care and drove to Newburgh to visit him. Ken died a few days later. I know the Spirit inspired Brother and Sister Stone to visit Ken on behalf of the Lord that day. Surely, the Lord Himself welcomed Ken home.

One wintry day, I got another glimpse of serving in the Lord's way. A young man in the ward scheduled his Eagle project for the Saturday before his eighteenth birthday. His project had to be completed before he turned eighteen to meet the requirements to become an Eagle Scout. He had planned to build a storage shed for a local town. Saturday came, and there was a blizzard. He could not reschedule the construction. The members of the ward and his family rallied around him. In the bitter cold and in a heavy snowfall, we joined together to build the shed. I loved it! We worked together in harmony without a single word of complaint. If I dropped a nail in the snow and I couldn't find it, no problem. If I hit my hand with the hammer, no problem. We were all there to support him to fulfill his dream of becoming an Eagle Scout. The joy and empowerment of service were clearly present.

In spite of all my training in serving in the Lord's way, I still frequently served as if I had a heavy load to bear. The Lord was inviting me to let Him share my burden, and I resisted. I couldn't see what was keeping me from partnering with Him. I longed for the lightness of being that I had observed in the service of my fraternity brothers at BYU. I aspired to have the joyful spontaneity Sister Avenius had in changing our door closer. Instead of being invigorated by my service, I often felt depleted. I began to look for ways to elevate my service so that it was empowering to both me and those I served.

Notes:

1. Davis, J. (1940). "You Are My Sunshine." New York: Peer International.

2. Norworth, J., & Tilzer, A. (1908). "Take Me Out to the Ball Game." Madison, WI: Musicnotes.

3. Berlin, I. (1938). "God Bless America." New York: Irving Berlin.

CHAPTER 32

THUNDER'S LASTING IMPACT

AS A RECENT convert, I listened as people prayed before meals. They often used the phrase, "Bless this food that it may nourish and strengthen our bodies." I started making the same appeal before my meals. As I ate, I wondered if the food I was eating provided the nourishment and strength I prayed for.

As if in response to my prayerful reflection, I received an assignment to be the home teacher of a member of our ward who was a nutritionist. After several home teaching visits, I made an appointment to consult with her about what I was eating. Under her guidance, I changed my diet, took the recommended supplements, and became more energetic. To my surprise, I went through an entire winter without getting a cold.

She advocated for minimizing exposure to toxins. As a preventative measure, she recommended removing the mercury fillings in my teeth and referred me to a dentist who replaced them with resin fillings. The dentist was an orthodontist. He noticed a misalignment in my jaw, and he told me the misalignment was affecting my entire skeletal structure. His comment piqued my interest. I had recurring back pain, and I saw realigning my jaw as a way to reduce my pain and the related stress.

This dentist also told me I needed to deal with some underlying structural issues before he could work on my jaw. He referred me to an acupuncturist, a chiropractor, and a physical therapist. On my first visit with the acupuncturist, he put a needle in my right hip and said, "You were injured here." He had inserted a needle where one of Thunder's hooves had left its mark when I was a boy. Even though the injury had taken place almost fifty years earlier, he could tell I had been injured by how I responded to the needle. I didn't realize my body had retained a memory of being kicked.

He explained, "Trauma needs to be released with proper care, or it remains locked in the body." He went on to say that animals die if they don't shake off trauma. He then said, "Humans tend to hold on to trauma, and it shows up in various forms of stress seemingly unrelated to the physical injury." I could see that I had to let go of that trauma or live with the effects of it.

The recommended physical therapist was a specialist in myofascial release. I told him about my childhood injury. He explained that his work freed the body from the effects of trauma stored in the myofascial tissue. In other words, as a result of stress, the fascia loses its natural slipperiness. His work was intended to restore the natural slipperiness to the fascia and to resolve stress related to physical injury.

After working with the physical therapist for several weeks, I went to the chiropractor. He asked me how I was feeling. I told him that I was an emotional wreck. The myofascial work had released emotions locked in my soft tissue, and I was emotionally sensitive. The chiropractor knew what to do. We began a series of treatments using various techniques to process my emotional stress. I continued to work with the physical therapist and the chiropractor for several months and then returned to the dentist. On the foundation of releasing physical and emotional stress, the dentist worked with me to realign my jaw. In the process, I had a greater sense of well-being. Nevertheless, I felt like there was more to be done.

At one point the chiropractor told me, "Once you release pent-up emotions, you need to reintegrate your energy around an empowered sense of yourself." I had been doubting my own value, and I had been using my service to convince myself I was a good person. I had released the negative emotions that supported my disempowered view of myself, and I began to look for a way to reintegrate my energy around a positive self-image.

As the next step, I started working with a psychotherapist who specialized in treating trauma. From her, I learned that healing from trauma is different than recovering from other psycho-emotional issues. Just talking about a traumatic incident can actually retraumatize a person. We took it slowly, and she had me recount details related to my injury rather than emotionally charged memories of it. With her coaching, I gained a positive view of myself. I was also able to resolve other lingering stressors, such as my failed attempt to go away to college when I was eighteen and my brother's death. This gave me the freedom to claim my identity as a son of God.

Through these various therapeutic modalities, I emerged at peace with myself. I was free to make mistakes, make corrections, and accept the love extended to me. As a bishop, when I met with ward members, I often told them, "The Lord loves you." Then I asked, "Are you ready to receive His love?" Finally, I was able to answer my own question and say, "Yes, I am ready."

My new-found freedom to accept the Lord's love made it possible to live my life as an integrated whole. As a young man, I had marveled that Mitch Hunt's faith in Christ was present in everything he did. When I joined the Church, Bishop Avenius impressed me with how he consistently expressed his faith at home, at church, and at work. My freedom in Christ enabled me to follow their examples!

I was genuinely alive in Christ. I no longer served as a way to fulfill an obligation and to provide evidence I was a good person. My service became a consistent expression of God's love. Now as I contribute to others, I bring vitality and spontaneity.

My confidence in my relationship with the Lord allowed me to see that I was cutting myself off from people I had known when I was in the Unification Church. Even though I had had many close friends in the Unification Church, I had ended those friendships when I joined the Church of Jesus Christ of Latter-day Saints. This was inconsistent with my commitment to having an embracing love for all people. When I saw what I was doing, I reached out to some of my Unification Church friends and reclaimed our friendship.

This resulted in an invitation to speak to a group of young Unificationists at the Unification Theological Seminary. I had not been in the building for more than a decade. In one of the lecture halls I had attended classes as a student, I shared several of my personal experiences with Reverend Moon. The enthusiastic expressions of gratitude for my short talk warmed my heart.

Afterward, I was standing by a table where I had put on display pictures of leaders I had worked with. Looking at the pictures, one young woman said, "That is my grandmother!" She was pointing to a picture of Mrs. Mose Durst who had been an inspiration to me when I was with the Oakland Family. When I joined the Unification Church, I had met her son Isaac, who was in his preteen years. It was wonderful to meet his adult daughter almost forty years later.

I can now enjoy my friendships with Unificationsts without concern for our religious differences. Even though I no longer revere Reverend Moon as providing the path for me to fulfill God's purpose for my life, I can embrace my time with the Unification Church. I will be forever grateful to Reverend Moon for serving on behalf of God to bring Alice and me together. I am also indebted to him for instilling in my heart a vision of the unity of all people centered on God.

My healing journey gave me a new appreciation for the personal hardships created by my childhood injury. As I lived with the effects of physical trauma, I developed as a person. Without that trauma, I would not be the man I am today. I see that my life has been blessed by this adversity, and I acknowledge the Lord for trusting that I would rise to the challenge and benefit from it.

CHAPTER 33

SAVIOR ON MOUNT ZION

WHEN I FIRST met the family history director in the Kingston Ward, he asked me, "Are you descended from George Bowers who emigrated from England to Massachusetts in the 1630s?"

I said, "Yes."

"We are cousins!" he exclaimed.

I had been baptized for only a few weeks, and here I was meeting an embracing distant cousin. How cool!

Even before I joined the Church, I had attempted to identify my ancestors. As a student at BYU, I attended a Sunday School class on genealogy. The instructor suggested that we talk to our grandparents and write down their stories while they were still living. With this in mind, on the next school break, I had a conversation with my mother's mother, Ruth Appelbe. I asked her if she knew anything about Grandpa Appelbe's family. She told me that right after World War II, Grandpa had received a letter from one of his cousins in England, who was a lawyer. She showed me the letter inviting my grandfather to go to England for a visit. This invitation became a link to his relatives.

In 1995, I was preparing to go to a conference in England sponsored by the Council for the World's Religions. I decided to see if I could meet some of my grandfather's relatives while I was there. I called one of my mother's cousins in Canada and asked her if she knew anyone in the Appelbe line in England. She said she did not. Then I asked her if she knew anything about our cousin who was a lawyer. My question reminded her she had met him, and she gave me his daughter's address. I wrote to her, and she invited me to come to her home while I was in England.

What a memorable meeting! She told me her grandfather had been a Methodist missionary to Botswana and showed me pictures of South Africa, where her father was born. She also said her grandfather had known Mahatma Gandhi when he had lived in South Africa. As a result of his acquaintance with her grandfather, Gandhi knew her father as a boy, and they had stayed in touch throughout Gandhi's life.

In his autobiography, Yogananda identified Gandhi as a modern saint. They met in India in the 1930s. During their time together, Gandhi asked Yogananda to teach him the Kriya Yoga meditation technique. I felt connected to Gandhi because of our common bond with Yogananda, and I delighted in the discovery that some of my relatives knew Gandhi personally.

The real bonus was that she took me to have lunch with her father, Ambrose Appelbe, who had written to my grandfather in 1945. Fifty years later, I arrived in response to his invitation. What a pleasure to meet him! He bore a striking resemblance to my grandfather. They both had big bushy eyebrows, a ruddy complexion, and a jovial demeanor. It was as if I was with my grandfather again. All this was possible because I had followed the suggestion of a Sunday School teacher to talk to my grandmother about our family when I was at BYU!

Growing up, I loved to hear the story of a defining choice my father's mother made on Tuesday, April 16, 1906. My father's family had arrived by train in Santa Rosa, California late in the day. All their furniture was in a boxcar, and their new home was completely empty. My grandfather asked my grandmother if she wanted to spend the night in the hotel. She said, "No, let's just take the mattresses out of the boxcar and sleep on the floor." I am glad they did. Early the next morning, the infamous San Francisco earthquake hit. Santa Rosa was actually the epicenter. The Santa Rosa Hotel where they would have stayed collapsed, and everyone in it died. If my grandmother had chosen to stay in the hotel, my father would never have been born. When I reflect on this story, I feel the watchful care of God.

I also heard inspiring stories about my great-grandfather, John Taylor Bowers. He left Greenfield, New Hampshire, for California in 1848 with two brothers and a sister. They arrived in August 1849, and John got a job with Wells Fargo as an express messenger. He carried gold dust from Sacramento to the United States Mint in San Francisco. This was a trip of over one hundred miles, made on horseback. It was a dangerous job. His safety depended on people knowing he was ready and able with his sidearms. He carried a pair of heavy revolvers, and he made an exhibition of his marksmanship whenever he could. Target shooting was a common sport, and there were plenty of opportunities to demonstrate his skill. His favorite trick was to tack a small playing card to a tree, then stand with his back to it for a few moments until he had an attentive audience. He then strode quickly away from the tree, counting his paces aloud. When he reached the count of twenty-five, he whirled around, drew, and shot all in one motion. In rapid fire, he consistently put five of the six bullets in the card. He became famous for this demonstration of marksmanship.

He typically carried $30,000 worth of gold dust in his saddlebags on his trips from Sacramento to San Francisco. In a ruse to deceive potential highwaymen, he would go into a saloon and pretend to get drunk. In the saloon, he bragged he was going to pick up a shipment of gold dust in the morning at the express office and carry it by horseback to San Francisco. He boasted he was ready for any bandits who might try to stop him. He put on a show of stumbling out of the saloon as if he were drunk. In fact, he was sober, and he had the gold dust with him in his saddlebags. When he left the saloon, he mounted his horse and safely rode through the night. As a boy hearing this story, I was proud of my great-grandfather's skill with a gun and his bravado in deceiving robbers who might have stolen the gold dust he carried.[1]

My great-grandfather had a good singing voice and knew all the popular tunes of the time. As he sat around campfires on the trail to California, he led people in song. Later in life, he often sang with family and friends around the piano in his home. I thought about my great-grandfather and his love for singing as I sang in my youth.

In June 1976, his youngest son died. On the day of Uncle Nate's funeral, I was on a Unification Church fundraising team in the San Francisco Bay Area. The team leader dropped me off at the funeral home. I was grateful I could attend the service. Uncle Nate was my childhood hero. He amazed me with his accomplishments. He had a PhD in civil engineering from Stanford University. He enjoyed a successful career as a journalist with an engineering magazine, he served as a correspondent during World War II, and he was an accomplished photographer. He was an inventor with several patents to his credit, and he was a respected expert on tree rings. I admired him for his achievements, but he captured my heart by the personal attention he gave me.

At the end of the funeral service, his caregiver arrived. While the rest of the family departed, she greeted me. I had been to visit Uncle Nate six months earlier. She said that when I came, he had been weak, and limited the time he let people stay with him. She had noticed he let me stay longer than other people, and when I left, he told her, "I let him stay because when I looked into his eyes, I saw my father's eyes." With those words, I completely broke down. My tears flowed as a sense of love and connection to my great-uncle and my great-grandfather washed over me.

When I joined the Church, I started looking for my ancestors with a new sense of purpose. When I found identifying information for them, I completed temple work on their behalf. In doing so, I made available to them a greater measure of God's love and mercy.

At first, I limited myself to looking for direct-line ancestors and their children.

The scope of my research expanded after I read a passage from a memoir written by one of my ancestors, Anson Green. Anson was a Methodist minister, and he told a story of running into a cousin at a church meeting in upstate New York. Before he saw her, she came through the crowd and threw her arms around him. They both rejoiced in their meeting.[2] After some research, I realized they were actually third cousins. At the time, my third cousins seemed like distant relatives.

As I pondered the meeting, the Spirit revealed to me that in the next world, there is a close family connection to third cousins. I then expanded my research to include anyone with whom I share a common ancestor and their spouses. I love affirming my relationship to my ancestors through temple work and sharing family history information with living relatives.

In 2006, it was time to be sealed to my parents. My father had died, and I had done all the preliminary temple work for both my father and my mother. All that remained was for me to request to be sealed to them. The prospect of living with them for eternity exposed hard feelings I had toward my mother because she disapproved of my choice to join the Unification Church. After several weeks of soul-searching prayer, Heavenly Father shared His heart with me. Through the whispering of the Spirit, He intimated that He had personally chosen my parents and that they had provided me with exactly the kind of parenting I needed. Moved that Heavenly Father had selected my parents and that He stood behind their parenting, I let go of my bitterness. With peace in my heart, I went to the temple to create an eternal bond with them. No words can describe the profound comfort I felt following the sealing ceremony. I was complete with the past and secure in our future together.

In April 2007, Alice, David, Patricia, and I attended the General Conference of the Church of Jesus Christ of Latter-day Saints in Salt Lake City. I had some time the day before the conference, and I went to the Family History Library. I walked into a large reading room, and on one wall there was a massive display of a family tree. At the bottom of the tree were the names of one couple. The tree listed the names of hundreds of their descendants, including Joseph Smith. I stepped closer and saw the couple at the root of the tree was Robert White and Bridget Allgar, who were married in England in 1585. I immediately recognized their names. They are my ancestors through Stella Morrison, my father's grandmother. I realized Joseph Smith, the first prophet of the Church, is one of my cousins. This discovery gave me a close feeling of kinship with him.

Joseph Smith's declaration of the value of the work we do in the temples of the Church empowers me to stay actively engaged in it. He said, "We become saviors on Mount Zion by performing sacred ordinances for the dead."[3] He explained that Jesus Christ, through his death and resurrection, did something for us we could not do for ourselves. By performing sacred temple ceremonies on behalf of our kindred dead, we do for them what they cannot do for themselves, and we contribute to their salvation. This is the fulfillment of the prophecy of Malachi that the hearts of the fathers will be turned to their children, and the hearts of the children will be turned to their fathers (Malachi 4:6).

Notes:

1. Bowers, N. (1963). *John Taylor Bowers: Biographical notes*. Unpublished.

2. Green, A. (1877). *The Life and Times of the Rev. Anson Green, D.D.* Toronto: The Methodist Book Room.

3. Teachings of the Presidents of the Church—Joseph Smith. (2007). Salt Lake City, Utah: The Church of Jesus Christ of Latter-day Saints.

CHAPTER 34

A REUNION OF PRAYER PARTNERS

IN MARCH 2013, I was serving in the Manhattan Temple. On a break, I shared with a friend about Bette Hunt. I told him, "When I came out of my last class of the day on Friday afternoon October 3, 1969, there was Sister Hunt. She had waited for me at the door to invite me to General Conference the next day." Then I said, "In all my years of schooling, no one else ever stood outside my classroom and waited to speak with me. In my mind, she sets the standard for sharing the gospel." I had told that story many times, and I didn't think much about telling it that day. When I got home, I found an email from Bette's daughter Rebecca. She said her mother had passed away early that morning. The Spirit let me know that the Lord had me share that story to celebrate Bette as the great missionary she was as she returned to live in His presence. It was His way of saying, "Well done, Bette!"

The Lord was watching over me when he had Bette wait for me outside my classroom and at many other times in my life. Usually, I was unaware of His presence. His watchful care began long before I prayed to get the part of Amahl. From the day I was born, He was working through the people and the events of my life to prepare me to embrace the gospel. My spiritual journey began as my grandmother read me Bible stories. My mother made her contribution by instilling in me the importance of regular church attendance. Through Scouting, the Lord taught me enduring values and the importance of service. The Lord worked through Yogananda to teach me the essentials of a disciplined, devoted life of faith. Emma Goddard, on behalf of the Lord, asked the fateful question, "Why don't you go to Brigham Young University?" At BYU, He provided me with the good companionship I sought. Through my Book of Mormon classes, He taught me that the Book of Mormon was a sacred book of scripture. The Lord also left me with an indelible memory of the testimonies of the leaders of the Church that they shared in the weekly devotional services at BYU.

Through Reverend Moon, the Lord brought Alice and me together and then blessed our union with our children, David and Patricia. The Lord used my commitment to interfaith work to prompt me to attend a meeting with President Hinckley at Madison Square Garden. The Savior worked through Sister Avenius to have Alice participate in a Joy School with Patricia, and He had Bishop Avenius expose my game of theological ping-pong. He inspired Carl to refer us to the missionaries, and He sent Elder Stokes and Elder Bundy to teach us. For over twenty years, the Savior repeatedly asked my college girlfriend to pray for me, and under His guidance, many friends joined us in the Jordan River Temple. Throughout my life, He has worked through countless people to minister to me. He has continued to guide me in discovering what it is to accept His love and find freedom in Him. He has kept his promise: "I will never leave you nor forsake you" (Hebrews 13:15).

My marriage to Alice was critical to His plan. Whenever people express surprise it took me so long to join the Church, Alice confidently explains, "He needed to meet me first!" There is no question about it. The Lord knew I needed someone who could transition with me to the Church of Jesus Christ of Latter-day Saints, and the Lord chose Alice to take that journey with me. He knew me, met me where I was, and worked to draw me to Himself. At the same time, He worked through me to open Alice's heart to the gospel.

In September 2014, I went to the Philmont Scout Reservation in Cimarron, New Mexico, for a leadership training. I arrived on Saturday, and I started looking for someone to go with me to church the next morning. At dinner, there were over two hundred Scout leaders in the dining hall. Among them, I was sure I could find a Latter-day Saint to attend church with me. I sat down at a table with some friends, and a man joined us. He introduced himself, and I asked, "Where are you from?" He said, "Ogden, Utah." When he finished his meal and got up to put his dishes away, I left the table with him and started a conversation.

"You said you are from Ogden—are you a member of the Church?"

He said, "Yes."

I asked, "Would you like to go to church with me in the morning?"

He responded, "I can't. My training starts right after breakfast."

We continued our conversation, and I asked him, "Did you attend the recent open house for the rededication of the Ogden temple?" He said he did, and he told me about some of the renovations.

I added, "I attended the open house for the Provo temple when I was a student at BYU."

He replied, "I went to the Provo temple open house too." We walked together to put our dishes away and said goodnight.

Walking back to my tent, I reflected on the fact we had both been at BYU at the same time. Then it dawned on me that he might be one of my friends from the sociology program who had prayed with me to know if the gospel was true in the early 1970s. The next morning, I saw him at breakfast and asked, "What did you study at BYU?" He said, "Sociology."

We immediately realized we were old friends. After the initial amazement, I asked him, "Do you remember fasting and praying with me that I might know the gospel was true?"

He said, "Yes, I remember well!"

The Lord brought us together again after more than forty years to remind us that He had not forgotten our prayer.

My journey continues in service to my family, church, and community. Along the way, the Lord stands ready to answer my prayers.

CPSIA information can be obtained
at www.ICGtesting.com
Printed in the USA
FFHW020850100519
52388957-57797FF